CONTEMPORARY EDITING WORKBOOK

BETH ROGERS THOMPSON
The Pennsylvania State University

BRAD THOMPSON
The Pennsylvania State University

NTC Publishing Group
a division of NTC/Contemporary Publishing Group
Lincolnwood, Illinois USA

Sponsoring Editor: Marisa L. L'Heureux
Editor: Lisa A. De Mol
Art Director: Ophelia M. Chambliss
Production Coordinator: Denise Duffy-Fieldman

ISBN (workbook): 0-8442-2346-8
ISBN (student text): 0-8442-3210-6

Literary acknowledgments begin on page 186, which is to be considered an extension of this copyright page. Photos are credited on the page on which they appear.

Published by NTC College Publishing,
a division of NTC/Contemporary Publishing Group, Inc.,
4255 West Touhy Avenue,
Lincolnwood (Chicago), Illinois 60646-1975 U.S.A.
© 2000 by NTC/Contemporary Publishing Group, Inc.
All rights reserved. No part of this book may be reproduced,
stored in a retrieval system, or transmitted in any form or by any means,
electronic, mechanical, photocopying, recording, or otherwise,
without prior permission of the publisher.
Manufactured in the United States of America.

90 VL 0 9 8 7 6 5 4 3 2 1

Contents

Introduction v

PART 1 APPROACHING THE STORY   1

Chapter 1	•	**3**	•	Developing the editor within
Chapter 2	•	**5**	•	Focus on news judgment: The editor's attitude
Chapter 3	•	**7**	•	Focus on skills: Tools of the editor
Chapter 4	•	**17**	•	Focus on grammar: The mechanics of language
Chapter 5	•	**31**	•	Focus on good writing: Strong and graceful prose

PART 2 INSIDE THE STORY   51

Chapter 6	•	**53**	•	News close to home: Editing local stories and community news
Chapter 7	•	**63**	•	News from afar: Editing wire stories
Chapter 8	•	**83**	•	Making a long story short: Editing for brevity and clarity
Chapter 9	•	**109**	•	After the fact: Editing features and more complex story structures
Chapter 10	•	**121**	•	No safety in numbers: Polls and survey stories
Chapter 11	•	**131**	•	Doing justice: Legal issues, ethics and bias

PART 3 BEYOND THE STORY   135

Chapter 12	•	**137**	•	Headlines: Precision, power and poetry
Chapter 13	•	**149**	•	An eye for news: Editing photos
Chapter 14	•	**157**	•	Showing the story: Editing information graphics
Chapter 15	•	**167**	•	The balancing act: Designing pages
Chapter 16	•	**177**	•	From gatekeeper to guide: Editing for online media

Appendix: Spring Valley City Directory 179
Acknowledgments 186

Introduction

This book is intended to help you prepare for a career in news copy editing. We know from years of experience on copy desks that the problems in the exercises are the same ones that come up frequently in copy editing. Although the Internet and the World Wide Web are revolutionizing communications, copy still needs to be edited. Even though home computers can run the same sophisticated layout software that major newspapers and magazines use, design still needs to be understood. Even so, editing for the Web is increasingly important, and the last chapter of this book should give you a basic understanding of differences between print and online editing. But we can't cover everything; there is no substitute for experience and judgment. What we have tried to give you is enough practice for you to know whether copy editing is a good career choice for you and — if you can correctly do these exercises — enough experience to get your first job. Whether in print or online, there will always be jobs for people who know the rules of language, headline writing and visual presentation. The information explosion will ensure that.

Since 1986, we have taught several hundred students copy editing, both at Penn State and at Metropolitan State College in Denver. Each of us has more than 15 years of news writing and editing experience, including stints as reporter, copy editor, slot, wire editor, assistant news editor, assistant city editor and section editor at the Greenville (S.C.) News, the Charlotte (N.C.) News, the Charlotte Observer and the Rocky Mountain News in Denver. In addition, we continue to do freelance editing and writing. We draw on this experience every day we teach and believe that it is reflected in this book.

We want to thank Marisa L. L'Heureux at NTC/Contemporary Publishing for asking us to write this book and Lisa A. De Mol for her expert supervision of us and the publishing process. We also want to thank NTC's copy editor on this project, Linda LiDestri. No one knows more than we that even copy editors need copy editors when they write. Although we worked independently from them, Cecilia Friend, Don Challenger and Kathy McAdams, the authors of this book's companion volume, *Contemporary Editing,* shared some of their thoughts and ideas with us. Finally, we want to thank our colleagues at Penn State and elsewhere for their help in this endeavor and throughout the years we have worked together.

If you have any questions or comments about the book, please contact us at the College of Communications, Penn State, University Park, PA 16802; by e-mail at wbt3@psu.edu; or by phone at (814) 865-1336.

Beth Rogers Thompson
Brad Thompson

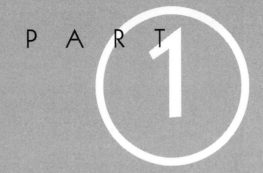

Approaching the Story

CHAPTER 1

Developing the Editor Within

Copy editors play a crucial role in determining the success of a newspaper, magazine or Web site. They make sure stories, headlines, photo captions and graphics are accurate and readable. Copy editors often work under tremendous deadline pressure, for after all, it doesn't matter if a publication consistently produces award-winning stories if that publication is consistently late arriving on readers' doorsteps or computer screens. Although the techniques and styles of copy editing have changed over the years, the fundamentals of ensuring quality and meeting deadlines have remained constant. The exercises in this chapter are designed to give insights on how copy editing fits into the operation of the newsroom. The exercises also introduce some of the skills that copy editing requires.

Exercises

1. Choose a locally written news story in a local newspaper or, if you are away from home, one from your hometown. Call or visit the city desk, and find out the name and position of each person who handled that story after the reporter turned it in and before it was set in type. If possible, get a copy of the reporter's unedited version, then explain how each person modified or otherwise handled the story.

   a. Who wrote the headline and/or photo captions that accompanied the story? Were these modified by the copy desk chief or another editor before reaching their final form?

   b. Talk to the writer, and get his or her reaction to the editing of that particular story. Were any errors injected along the way? Does the reporter think the headline accurately reflects the story?

   c. If the story had to be trimmed to fit the allocated space, does the reporter agree with how it was cut or have suggestions for more appropriate information that could have been omitted instead?

   d. If the story appeared in both print and on the Internet, were there any differences in the two versions? Explain in detail.

2. Go to the library and compare the front pages of today's edition of a nationally distributed newspaper such as The New York Times, Washington Post, Los Angeles Times or USA Today, and your local or hometown paper with editions of those newspapers from:

The day you were born;

The birth date of one of your parents;

The birth date of one of your grandparents.

For each of these front pages:

   a. Compare and categorize the number and types of stories.

   b. Describe the design, or appearance, of the page, and note, for example, the number of columns and the use, number and relative sizes of photographs and other art elements.

   c. Compare the headline characteristics: wording, relative sizes, the number of characters or words.

   d. List the sources used in the stories. Compare the representation of government officials, experts, other individuals and/or institutions. Note how information is attributed to these sources, including the use of words such as *said, says, claimed* and *according to*. Are anonymous sources used in any of the stories, and if so, how are the sources referred to?

   e. Compare the length (number of words and sentences) and style of language used in the lead paragraphs.

CHAPTER 2

Focus on News Judgment: The Editor's Attitude

An important skill for all journalists, perhaps especially copy editors, is to develop a sense of how a publication reflects and serves its community. This includes news judgments — not only considering the elements of news, such as timeliness — but also an understanding of the audience. What's interesting and relevant in one city may be of little or no concern in another. A particular event might be run as a long story that starts on page 1 in one newspaper, be reduced to a three-paragraph brief on an inside page in another, and not even be mentioned in a third paper. As an editor, you also must make judgments about headlines, layout, photos and graphics that enhance stories and give readers clues to their relative importance that day. The following exercises will give you a glimpse of these editing responsibilities.

Exercises

1. To get a closer look at the demands of copy editing, choose an editor at your local or hometown newspaper and spend part of a day with that person, observing the meetings he or she attends, the various tasks performed on the job and the interactions with reporters, copy editors and other staff members. Write a brief, hour-by-hour activity report of that person's day, commenting on what you observe.

2. Interview an editor or manager at your local or hometown newspaper about the copy-editing positions there. What skills are required? What qualities and experience does this particular publication look for when hiring a copy editor?

3. Look at three different newspapers from the same day: a nationally distributed newspaper, such as The New York Times, Los Angeles Times or USA Today; a major regional newspaper, such as the Boston Globe, Chicago Tribune, Denver Post, Philadelphia Inquirer or Portland Oregonian; and a local paper or your hometown paper. Compare and contrast:

   a. The top story of the day — differences in placement on the page, leads and headlines;

   b. Use of photos, graphics, maps and/or charts;

   c. Mix of local, regional, national and international news stories;

   d. Mix of wire news vs. staff-written stories.

4. In your local or hometown newspaper, find a story that has a weak or buried lead and rewrite it. How would you explain your changes if challenged by the reporter?

CHAPTER

Focus on Skills: Tools of the Editor

As a copy editor, you must ensure that each story reads well from beginning to end. This means checking to make sure every person in the story is fully identified (no last names without first names, for example); that the lead contains the appropriate information; that the story contains a "nut graf" if it doesn't begin with a traditional who-what-where-when summary lead; that there are no "holes," or missing details; and that transitions move the reader logically from one idea to the next. You should consult the reporter or assigning editor before making major changes, but sometimes you will need to do some rewriting and fact checking or even fact gathering to make stories accurate and complete.

Exercises

1. In the following three stories, one or more paragraphs appear out of sequence. In each story, rearrange and number the paragraphs so the story would flow more smoothly and logically. Make a note of the "clues" that tip you off to the correct arrangement, such as titles and names, first references or transitions.

    a. Sex shops

    State judges are continuing to label adult video stores and some strip clubs that limit pornography sales and nude dancing to less than 40 percent of their floor space as "nonadult," which enables them to remain open. But how long the businesses can withstand falling profits and rising legal costs remains to be seen.

    Since the crackdown began, 59 of the 144 strip clubs and adult video stores affected by a new zoning law have closed or shifted to nonadult entertainment, city officials say. But state judges have been upholding a legal strategy that has allowed many of the shops and clubs to stay open.

    Three months after a spate of padlockings heralded the arrival of a crackdown on New York City's sex shops by the administration of Mayor Rudolph W. Giuliani, a string of legal victories by adult business owners has turned what looked like a speedy rout into a war of attrition.

-30-

b. FedEx

Ballots will be sent this week to the 3,200 members of the FedEx Pilots Association. The union hopes to complete the balloting by Nov. 20.

The union said in a statement it was forced to take the vote because of a lack of progress in contract talks. The company's pilots, more than 90 percent of whom belong to the union, have never had a contract since they became unionized in 1993.

Leaders of the Federal Express pilots' union voted unanimously Sunday to seek strike authorization from members.

Under the proposal, total career earnings for a FedEx pilot would reach $9.1 million, while UPS fliers make $9.7 million, according to the documents.

The company also said the proposal would improve schedules, raise retirement benefits, keep the vacation plan and prohibit the company from using non-FedEx airplanes and crews to deliver cargo.

FedEx chief executive officer Ted Weise countered the company has a proposal on the table that would put pilots "in the very top echelon of the airline industry in every major category."

His comments were in a cover letter sent Saturday to pilots, along with copies of the latest contract offer and an actuarial study showing the total compensation package would move them from ninth in the industry to No. 2 behind UPS.

Union officials say the study is flawed and that the company wants pilots to work 8 percent more for a 4 percent pay increase.

The union's executive board already has sent ballots to pilots asking whether they would be willing to refuse to work overtime during the Christmas season. The results of that vote will be announced Thursday.

They say career compensation for FedEx pilots is 37 percent below their top rival United Parcel Service, while retirement compensation is 213 percent below United Airlines.

c. MS

In multiple sclerosis, the body's immune system attacks the protective sheath around nerve fibers. The three multiple sclerosis drugs approved in recent years work in various ways to trick the immune system into stopping or slowing the attack, Dr. Van den Noort said.

The National Multiple Sclerosis Society is urging anyone given a diagnosis of the disease to start drug treatment immediately rather than wait for symptoms to worsen.

Although medication exists to treat multiple sclerosis, fewer than 50,000 of the 300,000 Americans who have the often-crippling nerve disease are taking the three drugs that slow the progression of it but do not cure it, a society spokesman, Dr. Stanley van den Noort, said on Friday at the organization's leadership conference.

"Within 5 or 10 years, I suspect that we'll have something better," Dr. Van den Noort said. "But we don't know what it is. And this is the best thing we've got. And it's safe. And it works. It's not perfect, but it does reduce the attack rate, and . . . there's pretty good evidence that it does stop the accumulation of disability."

The society has provided only information about treatments in the past. It did not say which of the three available drugs – Avonex, Betaseron and Copaxone – is best, said Dr. Van den Noort, a neurology professor at the University of California at Irvine, and the society's chief medical officer.

But in its first treatment recommendation, the society said all multiple sclerosis patients should be on medication, since it appeared that those taking the medication would most likely suffer fewer disabling symptoms than those who did not.

Multiple sclerosis patients typically lose some problem-solving capacity and short-term memory. The majority end up in wheelchairs or need assistance with walking, Dr. Van den Noort said.

Each of the three drugs cost about $1,000 a month and must be injected weekly to daily.

Many doctors are still unfamiliar with the drugs because they have been available only since 1993. And there remain questions about the benefits of the drugs when weighed against their high cost, effort for the patient and discomfort.

-30-

2. Reorganize and edit the following story so that it flows more logically. Also, note any questions you would need to ask the reporter:

HealthSouth

BELLEFONTE, Pa. — Health care giant HealthSouth Corp., its CEO and his wife have filed a libel suit against a Penn State employee for the statements he allegedly wrote about them on a Yahoo! Inc. Web site. Two Miami attorneys for HealthSouth traced the messages to the Penn State e-mail address of State College resident Peter D. Krum. The suit was filed Wednesday in Centre County Court, about a month after the attorneys filed a subpoena to get Yahoo! to find out the message writer's identity.

Penn State spokesman Bill Mahon said Krum is listed as a food and beverage handler with Penn State Hospitality Services, which operates the Nittany Lion Inn and the Penn Stater Conference Center Hotel.

Fischman said Krum worked as a food service supervisor at HealthSouth Nittany Valley location from January 1995 to December 1997 before leaving voluntarily.

Krum had used the name Dirk Diggler—the name of the porn star character played by actor Mark Wahlberg in the movie *Boogie Nights*—in posting messages on the HealthSouth message board on the Yahoo! Finance Web site, according to the lawsuit.

Yahoo! is a global Internet media company headquartered in Santa Clara, Calif., that founded the first Web site for navigating the Internet. Its Yahoo! Finance site provides electronic message boards for anyone to discuss particular companies.

HealthSouth, based in Birmingham, Ala., is the parent company of HealthSouth Nittany Valley Rehabilitation Hospital in Pleasant Gap.

HealthSouth describes itself as the largest provider of outpatient surgery and rehabilitative health care, with more than 2,000 locations in all 50 states, the United Kingdom and Australia. It reported revenues of more than $2.8 billion for the first nine months of 1998.

The company's lawsuit asks for compensatory, punitive and special damages, plus attorneys' fees and costs, and other relief.

One of the 14 messages listed in the lawsuit said HealthSouth "will stop at nothing to maintain the image of a respectable company. They (dump) on their employees in the blink of an eye." Another calls the company's senior management "white trash" and calls it inept. Other messages listed in the lawsuit make references to sexual acts.

The lawsuit calls the statements "false and defamatory."

Many of the messages target HealthSouth Chief Executive Officer Richard Scrushy and his wife, Leslie Scrushy, who live in Birmingham.

"None of it's true," said Bruce D. Fischman, one of the Miami attorneys who filed the suit. "Richard and his wife don't even know this guy. The allegations that he makes about the company ... are absolutely inaccurate, and were stated to make people believe they were accurate. The only purpose of this could have been to cause harm to the Scrushys and to HealthSouth."

"I can assure you that Richard Scrushy and his wife found it horribly offensive and distressing," he said.

When asked about the lawsuit, Krum said, "I don't know anything about that," and declined to comment further.

Yahoo! spokeswoman Diane Hunt said the company doesn't comment on specific cases and said the company only releases a Web user's personal information if it receives a court order or subpoena.

She said the company requires a verifiable e-mail address for all users of the Yahoo! Finance Web site. The terms and conditions of Yahoo! message boards instruct users not to send any messages that are "abusive, harassing, tortuous, defamatory, vulgar, obscene (or) libelous," among other warnings. Hunt said someone could "potentially" sign up for a message board and start sending messages without reading the terms and conditions.

Messages on the Internet, as short-lived as they may be, are still considered published statements under libel and defamation law, said Clay Calvert, a professor of communications and law at Penn State and co-director of the Pennsylvania Center for the First Amendment.

"The key thing for publication to occur is that one person other than the parties to the case read" the message, he said, adding that he was speaking generally and had not seen the HealthSouth lawsuit. "Libel may occur on the Internet, just like it can in any other medium," he said.

The lawsuit says the statements would make HealthSouth's customers "lose faith in the operations, integrity and financial soundness of HealthSouth."

Robert A. Martin, a Bellefonte attorney representing HealthSouth in the case, said the statements against Richard and Leslie Scrushy could have the same effect.

"Certainly, defaming principals in the company has to have an effect on the perception of the company," he said. "It's pretty hard to separate the two."

"I think you have to look at all the statements in their entirety, rather than one in particular," he said.

"If you went around and put up posters on telephone poles ... defaming someone, there is no privilege to do that," Martin said. "It's still in the public domain, it's just another means of communicating."

The HealthSouth lawsuit mentions no motive for the electronic messages.

Libel suits for Internet communication are "becoming increasingly common as more and more people use the Internet. It's really amounting to pouring new wine into old bottles. The same (legal) principles will probably apply."

Calvert said that one example of a libel lawsuit being filed on Internet communication is the recent suit filed against cyberjournalist Matt Drudge by White House staffer Sidney Blumenthal. The Blumenthal lawsuit, which is still being litigated, claims Drudge made defamatory statements about Blumenthal's personal life.

Drudge's Web site, "The Drudge Report," was the first media outlet to publish information about the Bill Clinton–Monica Lewinsky scandal.

-30-

3. You are editing a story about the representative from your congressional district who is campaigning for re-election. The representative's age given in the story seems too young — off by perhaps as much as 10 years, you suspect. The reporter has left for the day and cannot be reached. How could you determine the representative's correct age?

4. Use the telephone book, almanac, the Internet and/or other resources to find the information listed below. Also indicate the exact source of the information, such as title, edition, page number, etc.

  a. The population of your hometown: _____

  b. The birthplace(s) and age(s) of the U.S. senators from your home state: _____
  _____

  c. The seating capacity of the National Football League stadium nearest to you: _____

d. The name and location of an ethnic-food restaurant in your town, or a nearby town: _____
_____

e. The location of the nearest post office that accepts passport applications: _____

f. The correct spelling of the corporate name:
dupont
DuPont
Dupont
duPont

g. Wisconsin's state nickname: _____

h. The year Wyoming was granted statehood: _____

i. The number of congressional representatives from the state of New York: _____

j. The number of World Series titles the Atlanta Braves have won: _____

5. Use the correct proofreaders' symbols (found in the back of *The Associated Press Stylebook and Libel Manual*) to edit the following:

a. Most leads are limited to one sentence, and each paragraph should be limited to one idea. Choose one of the two symbols to indicate a new paragraph should start at the beginning of this sentence.

b. Sometimes a reporter takes the admonition to use short paragraphs too seriously and will unnecessarily divide one idea into two paragraphs.

c. Use the correct symbol to indicate this sentence and the one above belong in the same paragraph.

d. How could you these words transpose?

e. Circle spelled-out numbers, such as twenty, to indicate numerals should be used instead.

f. Similarly, you should circle a numeral, such as 2, to indicate it should be spelled out, when appropriate.

g. Also, you can circle a full name, such as United States Department of Agriculture, when you want to abbreviate it, or circle an abbreviation, such as NTSB or FAA, to indicate it should be spelled out on first reference.

h. Draw three lines under a letter or word, such as maryland or aids, to make it uppercase.

i. Draw a slash through the capital letter starting a common noun, such as Physician, to indicate it should be lowercase.

j. Use an arch, or linking sym bol, to indicate a space should be eliminated.

k. Use either a zigzag markor a straight lineto indicate a space should be inserted.

l. Although you should edit in erasable pencil, you can use the word "stet" if you change your mind about an edit. This mark means to return to the original version of the text.

m. Use a caret to insert missing lettrs or words.

n. Mark a line or a delete symbol through extraa letters or or words.

o. Use reversed brackets to indicate text should be centered, and a regular bracket for indenting from either the right or left.

p. Insert an "equals" symbol when you need a hyphen to link letters or phrases. This symbol also makes certain words with prefixes easier to read, such as the often used term reelection.

q. Use a goal post symbol to indicate em dashes as opposed to hyphens should be inserted.

r. Please use a reverse caret above the line to insert quotation marks around my words, the instructor told the class.

s. Insert an apostrophe in the word when its a contraction but not when its a possessive pronoun.

t. Use either a bold dot or an X in a circle to insert a period in an abbreviation or at the end of a sentence, and use either the space symbol (#) or the symbol -30- to indicate the end of the story

CHAPTER 4

Focus on Grammar: The Mechanics of Language

It almost goes without saying that good grammar, word usage and punctuation are fundamental to any type of writing, whether it's a breaking news story or the great American novel. It's not just a matter of nitpicking or earning the approval of a fussy schoolmarm. It's really a matter of clarity. As a copy editor, you fine-tune the copy, ensuring that words are used correctly and precisely to avoid ambiguity and that the style is consistent. You also must make sure that transitions and punctuation effectively guide the reader through well-organized information, and signal shifts in topics, thoughts or tone. Some practices, such as the omission of the serial comma before *and* in a simple series, apply mainly to journalistic writing. The following exercises are designed to help you brush up on grammar and to alert you to many of the types of errors you're likely to encounter in copy editing.

Exercises

1. Some grammatical errors occur because the writer was unsure of the word's role in the sentence. It makes a difference, for example, whether you're using a word as a possessive pronoun (such as *its*) or a subject-verb contraction (*it's*). In the sentences below, identify the parts of speech: nouns, pronouns, verbs, adjectives and adverbs, prepositions and conjunctions.

    a. The sick dog laid its head gently in my lap.

    b. Our mother bakes the best apple pie in the world, but her cooking generally is mediocre.

    c. A physician has to attend school for many years before opening a practice.

    d. Although we like football, we do not have season tickets.

    e. While the committee presented its findings, the company chairman scowled at the members.

    f. The search committee has narrowed the choices for a new dean to eight candidates.

g. John did not mind Sally's yawning loudly, but her snoring kept him awake.

h. The homecoming queen was chosen by the student body.

i. You should conduct yourself professionally during a job interview.

j. Baking a homemade pizza surely beats ordering one from the deli.

2. *Who* often comes first when listing the "five W's and H" (*who, what, where, when, why* and *how*) of news writing, especially if the news concerns a prominent individual or organization. Common nouns, which are not capitalized, are the general descriptions of things and people. Proper nouns, always capitalized, are the specific names. Confusion usually arises over possessives and plurals, including their punctuation and subject-verb agreement. In each of the following examples, make corrections as needed. If the sentence is correct as it is, mark OK in front of it.

a. Politics is a topic that can be dangerous to bring up at a party.

b. Twenty-five bushels of wheat are enough to feed a large group.

c. Officials say 40 pounds is the minimum weight at which a child should graduate from a car seat to a seat belt.

d. Elaine left her newspaper job to write childrens' books.

e. More companys are offering benefits to same-sex couples.

f. A couple of birds were singing outside my window this morning.

g. An older couple were walking hand-in-hand down the street.

h. The mediocre student was relieved to receive all Cs for the semester.

i. Economics are a major concern for the new administration.

j. The event is open to all alumna of the University of Maryland.

k. People like to say the media is responsible for many of society's ills.

l. One criteria for the scholarship is financial need.

m. A number of students were upset about the exam schedule.

n. The number of bank failures have risen in recent years.

o. "Margin of error" is one phenomena about public-opinion polls that can be confusing.

p. The Rogers are putting their house up for sale this summer.

q. The Board of Directors have not approved the proposal to build a new plant.

r. A drunken driver ran into a car parked outside the Joneses' house.

s. The Smith's, who live across the street, heard the crash and ran out to inspect the damage.

t. Tornadoes can strike suddenly, allowing little time to prepare.

u. Attorney generals in several administrations disagreed on the spirit, as well as the letter, of the law.

v. The woman intensely disliked both of her daughters-in-law.

w. The courtroom had been the scene of many court-martials.

x. The Board of Trustees has approved a 5 percent across-the-board raise for faculty.

y. Economics are a major concern for politicians as the next election approaches.

3. Pronouns can cause confusion in several ways. Sometimes a contraction (*you're*) is mistakenly used in place of a possessive pronoun (*your*), for example. And there's something called pronoun-antecedent agreement. That means a company or a committee is *it*, not *they*, when referred to by a pronoun later in the sentence or paragraph. And even many good writers struggle with *who* vs. *whom*, a situation in which understanding sentence structure — whether the word in question is used as a subject or object — comes in handy. In each case, circle the correct choice.

   a. The jury has not returned [their / they're / it's / its] verdict yet.

   b. The automaker is recalling one of [their / they're / it's / its] new models.

   c. Every reporter at some point in [their / they're / his or her] career must decide whether to use anonymous sources.

   d. My daughter objects to [me / my] entering her room when she's away.

   e. I don't think John would mind [you / your / you're] taking a look at his story.

   f. The copy-desk chief objected to [his / him] chewing tobacco on deadline.

   g. I doubt that [me / my] giving any advice would change your mind.

   h. Smith said the [council / council's] voting to close the street was an example of [its / it's / them / they're / their] ignoring residents' wishes.

   i. L.L. Bean sent out [it's / its / their / they're] Christmas catalogs earlier last year.

   j. [Its / It's] a good policy to disconnect garden hoses before the temperature drops.

   k. [You're / your] likely to regret drinking that espresso just before bedtime.

   l. Nike defended [it's / its / their /they're] decision to use smaller swooshes on products.

4. In each case, circle the correct choice.

   a. Police are seeking the man [that / who / whom] fled from the scene.

   b. The woman [that / who / whom] police arrested Tuesday is also accused of forgery.

   c. The manager wanted to see [whoever / whomever] failed to arrive for work on time.

   d. Please give the package to [whoever / whomever] answers the door.

   e. It's a shame that [whoever / whomever] called didn't leave a message.

   f. No matter [who /whom] the prize goes to, it was a fair contest.

   g. Regardless of [who /whom] wins the lottery, there will be a big payoff.

   h. People [who / whom / that] litter create eyesores and health hazards.

   i. The forum featured nine candidates [who / whom / that] are running for state and local posts.

   j. I opened the newspaper Sunday and [who / whom] did I see smiling at me, but my brother.

   k. Depending on [who/whom] you believe, the woman could have died accidentally.

   l. Despite good intentions regarding diversity, the people most like ourselves are often the ones with [who / whom] we feel most comfortable.

5. In each case, circle the correct choice. Remember to use commas to set off nonessential clauses.

   a. The new reporter turned in a fire story [which / that] was far too long.

   b. Bridge is a game [which / that] is easy to learn but difficult to master.

c. The 25-year-old Pittsburgh man faces charges [which / that] stem from the hit-and-run death of a police officer.

d. Thieves attempting to siphon oil from a pipeline in Nigeria sparked a fire [that /which] killed at least 250 people near Lagos.

e. The military leader is being protected in Pakistan by Taliban, a Muslim militant group [that / which] controls 90 percent of Afghanistan.

f. Most readers prefer news stories [which / that] are clearly written and informative.

g. The doctor said several factors are associated with diabetic retinopathy [which / that] leads to vision loss.

6. When children first learn to talk, they naturally assume all verbs are "regular"; that is, that the past tense is formed by adding -ed. So, a 3-year-old says she "singed" a new song at day care, where she also "sitted" beside her best friend. We soon learn that *sing-sang-sung* and *sit-sat-sat* are only a few of the irregular verbs in English. But some of these verbs, such as *lie-lay-lain* vs. *lay-laid-laid,* continue to confuse us. The following exercises involve choosing from verbs easily confused or nouns easily confused with verbs, and choosing the correct forms. In each case, circle the correct word.

a. A good editor will [advice / advise] but not dictate.

b. My father likes to say that a wise man doesn't need [advice / advise], and a fool won't take it.

c. Free [advice / advise] is often worth the price.

d. I would [advice / advise] reporters not to rely on anonymous sources.

e. The exhausted miner [lay / laid / layed] down for a nap after his shift.

f. Police found the robbery suspect's I.D. [laying / lying] in the street.

g. Fund-raisers insist the scandal has not had a dampening [affect /effect] on contributions.

h. One longtime Democratic fund-raiser from Chicago said the scandal might discourage some voters but probably would not [affect /effect] fund raising.

i. People often have specific personal reasons for donating money to a candidate, and such reasons are unlikely to be [affected / effected] by the president's behavior.

j. Libel suits can have a chilling [affect / effect] on reporting.

k. The player's suicide deeply [affected / effected] his teammates.

l. Recent bombings are likely to [affect / effect] the peace process.

m. If politicians really want to [affect / effect] change, they can begin with campaign finance reform.

n. The weather often [affects / effects] plans for a space shuttle launch.

o. Council members feared closing the street would negatively [affect / effect] traffic flow.

p. International monitors have arrived to [insure / ensure / assure] that the Serbs comply with the deadline for troop withdrawal.

q. The speaker [insured / ensured /assured] students in the audience that writing skills are essential.

r. The high school is installing metal detectors in an effort to [insure / ensure / assure] safety.

s. It's less expensive to [insure / ensure] your car if you have a clean driving record.

t. Sobbing tourists [lay /laid] flowers, wreaths and cards on the marble steps at the Capitol the next morning.

u. The woman said she [lay / laid] down, fell asleep and missed her appointment.

v. The woman, who had stalked several entertainers, [lay / laid] her head on the railroad tracks as a train approached.

w. Neighbors said the unemployed woman had been depressed before she apparently [lay / laid] her two young sons on a bed and shot each of them before turning the gun on herself.

x. The speaker [sat / set] his notes on the lectern and grinned at the audience.

y. The officer remembered leaving his gun [sitting / setting] on the desk at home.

7. Most of the time, we don't have much difficulty getting subjects and verbs to agree: singular subject, singular verb; plural subject, plural verb. But some sentences trip us up, particularly those that involve prepositional phrases, clauses or a singular noun that "sounds" as if it should be plural. For example, *90 cents* might appear to be plural; after all, it ends in *–s*. But you wouldn't say that 90 cents are a lot to pay for a candy bar, would you? This is called a *collective* — it indicates one price. Similarly, *5 pounds* is one weight; *Five pounds is not hard to lose.* Confusion also can be created when the subject of the sentence contains both plural and singular nouns. In that case, the noun closest to the verb governs the singular/plural choice. In each case, circle the correct word.

   a. Either of the proposed parking options [is / are] likely to bring an outcry from neighbors.

   b. Neither the mayor nor the City Council members [see / sees] the need for more zoning restrictions in that neighborhood.

   c. Neither the Council members nor the mayor [were / was] at the blood drive.

   d. When a rash of school-violence incidents [occur / occurs], the public wonders what is wrong with today's youth.

   e. One of the people who [work / works] in the lab complained of unsanitary conditions.

   f. She is the only one of those chefs who [insist / insists] on keeping recipes secret.

   g. A number of seniors [have / has] decided not to take the final exam.

h. The number of people investing in the stock market [continue / continues] to rise.

i. The five acres in question [is / are] part of a larger area the family plans to sell.

j. Fifty miles [is / are] a long way to drive to see a movie.

k. A series of news stories [is examining / are examining] the effects of welfare reform.

l. Luke is part of the group that [has / have] decided to skip graduation.

8. Other verb forms also can cause confusion. Grammarians use the term *subjunctive mood* to describe the verb in sentences expressing a wish or other statement contrary to fact: If John *were* (not *was*) a woman, he'd be proud of his long eyelashes. Verbals (gerunds, infinitives and participles) look and sound like verbs but serve as nouns or adjectives in a sentence. Gerunds end in *–ing;* for example, Running *is the players' primary exercise during the off-season.* In this case, *running* is the subject of the sentence. Infinitives — "to" plus a verb, such as *to run* — can serve as nouns, adjectives or adverbs. It's important to recognize these different forms and their roles to ensure the correct verbs are chosen and that sentences are structured properly. Edit the following sentences as needed. If a sentence is correct as is, mark it OK.

    a. If I was rich, I would move to Paris and buy my parents a new home.

    b. Even if every politician was guilty of lying, democracy would still survive.

    c. The coach said if Smith was the only player taking steroids, she would simply kick her off the team.

    d. The witness said she wished it were possible to take back the statement she had made during the deposition.

    e. At home, the senator likes to read books, to watch television and playing with his grandchildren.

    f. Swinging like monkeys were the favorite playground pastime for the neighborhood children.

    g. She did not like him driving fast or especially to smoke in the car.

    h. Hiking and cycling were the physics professor's favorite outdoor activities. Longing to shed pounds after a long winter of being sedentary.

9. Conjunctions and prepositions are like a glue that binds sentences together and helps them flow. Problems occur in deciding whether to use *which* (when the meaning of the sentence is complete without the phrase it introduces) and *that* (when the meaning depends on the phrase it introduces). Remember, too, that an adjective describes a noun or pronoun; an adverb describes a verb, adjective or another adverb. These parts of speech, judiciously placed, can add color but should be used sparingly in news writing. Circle the correct choice in each of the following examples:

   a. Sammy Sosa of the Chicago Cubs sent money and supplies to his homeland, Dominican Republic, much [like / as] former Pittsburgh Pirate Roberto Clemente did for earthquake victims in Nicaragua.

   b. Texas Gov. George Bush could captivate the public, much [like / as] President Clinton could.

   c. The governor has been unable to muster support on controversial issues [like / such as] his school-voucher plan.

   d. The borough would like to impose a tax on unearned income from service businesses [like / such as] apartment rentals.

   e. The theme of the event was promoting unity [among / between] people of different religious denominations.

   f. Journalists and politicians are different today [from / than] their Watergate-era counterparts.

   g. Senior faculty members differed [from / with] the dean regarding the curriculum changes.

   h. Republicans differ [from / with] Democrats in style and ideology.

   i. I feel [bad / badly] about your failing grade, but you seem to be taking it [calm / calmly].

   j. The students felt [as if / like] the semester would never end.

10. In each of the following examples, edit the sentence so the word "only" appears in the correct place.

    a. Humor only works in advertising certain types of products.

b. A business that makes $1 million a year only has to pay $1,500 for the business privilege tax.

c. He says he believes that closet homosexuals only live that way because they are not satisfied with who they are.

d. We only go to church on Sundays, but our neighbors go several nights a week.

e. The store owner saw that the child only had 50 cents in his hand.

f. The woman's refrigerator only contained a pound of hamburger.

g. Supervisors at the company only docked the workers' pay if they were five minutes late.

h. You only have two options: leave or stay.

11. Rewrite the following sentences to make them complete rather than fragments, eliminate misplaced or dangling modifiers or otherwise make them read more smoothly.

    a. It is the first time Sosa went without a home run in four games since mid-August.

    b. An example of this type of humor would be if someone slipped on a banana peel, it would be hysterical, but if you personally slipped on one, it wouldn't be that funny anymore.

    c. Although downgraded to a tropical depression, the damage was still great.

    d. Born in Mississippi in 1931, James Earl Jones' life and career have led him through many changes.

    e. A winner of four Emmy awards and two Tony awards, Jones' roles include Darth Vader in *Star Wars*.

    f. She was also a graduate of Princeton in 1982, where she earned a bachelor's degree in microbiology.

g. First used in the 1960s, by 1985 the American Association of Suicidology listed 614 agencies that provided crisis hotlines.

h. Like a mother in the 1960s, who worries about her son hanging around with those long-haired boys, Joe says he was hanging out with the wrong crowd.

i. Although Glenn's first launch was not covered by so many reporters, which is not to say it went unnoticed.

j. Ambulances stood by in case the protest resulted in bloodshed. In addition, extra police on alert.

12. The role of punctuation is to signal links, pauses and stops to the reader. You could think of certain punctuation marks as corresponding to certain traffic signals: A comma indicates a pause, or yield; a period indicates a full stop. Hyphens link letters and words; dashes and parentheses (which should be used sparingly if at all) set off ideas for emphasis. Semicolons can take the place of conjunctions in linking complete thoughts; they also are useful to separate groups of names or items in a lengthy series that also includes commas. Colons alert readers to a list or statement that follows. If it's a complete sentence, you capitalize the word immediately following the colon; if it's a phrase or list, you use lowercase. In general, we use less punctuation in news writing; for example, we omit the serial comma before the word *and* in a simple series. And by all means, avoid the temptation of many beginning copy editors to insert quotation marks every time you see the word *said*. Often, it's an indirect quote. In the following examples, add, delete or correct punctuation and/or capitalization as needed.

   a. Norma McCorvey, or Jane Roe", was the anonymous woman in the Roe vs. Wade case.

   b. Sam Donaldson, an ABC News correspondent for more than 30 years will not say whether he wears a toupee.

   c. The victim, 19 was on his way home from work when the accident occurred.

   d. Rescue officials said the blaze which started Saturday apparently killed mostly villagers and farmers.

   e. "The Catholics are nonviolent," McCorvey said, "There is no storming into an abortion clinic or chaining people to staircases."

f. A high percentage of award winning commercials involve humor.

g. You must remember this: A kiss is still a kiss, a sigh is still a sigh.

h. That reporter is skilled at incorporating slice of life stories into her articles.

i. The speaker told the audience she was a second generation Korean American.

j. A 38 year veteran of political reporting he had covered Watergate and the fall of the Berlin Wall.

k. "I have decided not to veto the Council's decision", the mayor said.

l. Have you ever seen the movie version of "Amadeus?"

m. Its a shame the family could not get together for a reunion at Christmas.

n. Survivors included two daughters Ann Smith of Ann Arbor Mich. and Cecilia Rogers of Lakewood Colo. a son Charles Adams of Bristol Tenn. and five grandchildren.

o. The children decided not to go sledding, it was too windy and cold.

p. "Regardless of what happens", the president said "I refuse to resign".

q. Joan did not get the job she was overqualified.

r. We could have used your batting skill on the team, we lost by one run.

s. The accident occurred Nov. 19, 1996 near Detroit.

t. The author was born in Missoula, Mont. but the family moved to Minnesota when she was 3.

u. She said her favorite colors were purple, pink, and yellow.

v. During that harsh winter many of the villagers died of starvation.

w. The dean said, the professors should try to turn in their final grades earlier.

x. The victim was a 13 year-old resident of Salt Lake City according to police.

y. It's not unusual to receive a 10 to 20-year prison sentence for that offense.

CHAPTER 5

Focus on good writing: Strong and graceful prose

One of your responsibilities as a copy editor is to ensure consistency in style, whether your organization follows the Associated Press rules or has its own style guide. In many cases, for example, different spellings are acceptable; you must determine which is the preferred spelling for your publication and adhere to it. The most common style questions involve abbreviations, addresses, capitalization, datelines, dates and numbers. But you will find a wealth of other information in your stylebook as well.

Exercises

1. Correct the style errors as needed in the following sentences:

   a. Chief Executive Officer Jim West has named John Norman the Vice President and Worldwide Creative Director for the advertising agency.

   b. That quarterback was the Number One draft pick last season.

   c. Great achievements, as well as conflict, marked the Twentieth Century.

   d. Only one per cent of the contributions support the charity's administration.

   e. The speaker was active in both the Civil Rights Movement and the Women's Movement.

   f. People will remember the Clinton Administration for its many scandals, although the President also managed to accomplish quite a bit.

   g. The series continues February 8, when former surgeon general Joycelyn Elders speaks on campus.

h. Federico Peña, the former Mayor of Denver, went to Washington as Transportation Secretary.

i. He said he had not read James Fallows's book "Breaking the News."

j. The meeting will be held in October, 1999 in Los Angeles, CA.

k. [in a story to be published within seven days of the incident]
45 people were killed in the plane crash on Monday, October 5.

l. The Dow Jones Industrial Average declined 2% in 1997.

m. Governor Tom Ridge signed the legislation into law Tuesday.

n. The child was three years old when her oldest sister, Jane, died.

o. The fire broke out at 9:00 AM in the abandoned building at 101 East Elm Street.

p. Tarzan, a ten year-old Bassett Hound, ran away Sunday.

q. The teacher told her 8 AM class that students could easily check facts on that website.

r. [in a story appearing a day after the meeting]
Rick Smart testified Wednesday, October 14 before the borough council.

s. "Everyone is eager to reach a budget agreement," said Senator Trent Lott, Republican Mississippi.

t. Matthew Shepard, 21, died after 5 days on life support at a hospital in Fort Collins, Colo.

2. Circle the best choice in each case.

a. He lives at [1400 Oak Avenue / 1400 Oak Ave. / 1400 South Oak Ave.]

b. She lives on [East Second Street / E. 2nd St. / East Second St.]

c. Many people would like to see [General / Gen.] Colin Powell run for President.

d. The instructor obtained the [median / mean / average] score by adding all the scores and dividing by the number of students.

e. The toddler fell and cut himself on the [cement / concrete] sidewalk.

f. The [judge / Judge] said he was not [convinced / persuaded] of the man's guilt.

g. Before anyone noticed any smoke or flames, the blaze was well [underway / under way].

h. The playoffs will feature the Miami Dolphins [versus / V. / vs.] the Buffalo Bills.

i. The reporters [xeroxed / photocopied / Xeroxed] the documents.

j. Postal workers said the letters lacked [ZIP codes / Zip Codes / zip codes].

3. Circle the number of the best choice in each case.

   a. i. The woman's social security check was late this month.
      ii. The woman's Social Security check was late this month.
      iii. She opposes Britain's proposed social security program.
      iv. Both ii and iii are correct.

   b. i. He was traveling north from Chicago to Pontiac, Mich.
      ii. He was traveling North from Chicago, Illinois, to Pontiac, Michigan.
      iii. He was traveling north from Chicago, Ill., to Pontiac, Mich.
      iv. All are incorrect.

   c. i. For more information call 814-555-4806.
      ii. For more information call (814) 555-4806.

   d. i. The Legislature passed the bill at 11 p.m. Monday night.
      ii. The Legislature passed the bill at 11:00 p.m. Monday.
      iii. The Legislature passed the bill at 11 PM Monday.
      iv. The Legislature passed the bill at 11 p.m. Monday.

   e. i. Secretary of State Madeleine K. Albright had just returned from the Middle East.
      ii. Madeleine K. Albright, secretary of state, had just returned from the Middle East.
      iii. Both are correct.
      iv. Neither is correct.

f. i. The club's office is in Room 6.
  ii. The club's office is in Room Six.
  iii. The club's office is in room 6.

g. i. The doctor prescribed Vitamin A.
  ii. The doctor prescribed vitamin A.
  iii. The doctor prescribed vitamin-A.

h. i. The United Nations Security Council meets today.
  ii. The UN Security Council meets today.
  iii. The U.N. Security Council meets today.

i. i. We went skiing in the Sierra Nevada Mountains.
  ii. They went rafting on the Rio Grande River.
  iii. They went rafting on the Rio Grande.

j. i. Janet Jones, a University of Maryland alumni, has a master's degree in journalism from Columbia.
  ii. Janet Jones, a University of Maryland alumnus, has a Master's degree in Journalism from Columbia.
  iii. Janet Jones, a University of Maryland alumna, has a master's degree in journalism from Columbia.

k. Between Christmas and New Year's Day, most people gain at least
  i. five pounds.
  ii. 5 pounds.
  iii. 5 lbs.

l. An accident occurred at
  i. 4th and Iowa streets.
  ii. Fourth and Iowa streets.
  iii. Fourth and Iowa Streets.

m. i. Storms battered the midwest.
  ii. Storms battered several Midwestern states.
  iii. He drove west toward Pittsburgh.
  iv. Both ii and iii are correct.

n. i. Her birthday is in February.
  ii. Her birthday is Feb. 9.
  iii. Both are correct.
  iv. Neither is correct.

o. i. Daylight-saving time begins in spring.
ii. Daylight Savings Time begins in Spring.
iii. Daylight Saving Time begins in spring.

p. i. The campus store discounts it's t-shirts 25 per cent.
ii. The campus store discounts its T-shirts 25%.
iii. The campus store discounts its T-shirts 25 percent.

q. i. 12 noon
ii. noon
iii. 12:00 p.m.
iv. 12:00 noon

r. i. a 5-year-old judicial ruling
ii. a five-year-old judicial ruling
iii. a five year old judicial ruling

s. i. The Monongahela and Allegheny Rivers form the Ohio River.
ii. The Monongahela and Allegheny rivers form the Ohio River.

4. Circle the word or phrase that conforms to Associated Press style.

   a. The bill was co-sponsored by [Sens. / Senators / senators] Bill Owens and Dottie King.

   b. The [Senator / senator / Sen. / sen.] called the meeting to order.

   c. The doctor lives at 411 Bird [St. / Street] in Lake City, [Fla. / FL/ Florida].

   d. The accident occurred at [E. / East] [Seventh / 7th] [St. / Street] and Constitution [Ave. / Avenue].

   e. The bunting had the same red, [white, / white] and blue colors as the flag.

   f. The meeting will be held in October [, 2000 / 2000 / , 2000,] in [New Orleans. / New Orleans, La. / New Orleans, LA.]

   g. The fire left [4 / four] people dead and [12 / twelve] seriously injured.

   h. [45 / Forty-five] people died in the fiery plane crash.

   i. An ambulance was dispatched to [Two / 2] Dickinson [Drive / Dr].

   j. [The New York Times / "The New York Times"] is one of the most respected newspapers in the world.

5. Edit — but do not rewrite — the following passages, making any needed corrections in style, grammar and punctuation.

   a. Colombo is the capitol of Sri Lanka.

   b. The Congressional delegation met the counsel generals from Cameroon, Belize, and the Bahamas.

   c. The Philadelphia Metropolitan Area is comprised of the City of Philadelphia plus several suburbs in Pa. and N.J.

   d. Members of the Republican block of the city council and Blair County Commissioner John Arrington were among those who addressed the issue at Greenville city hall on Monday.

   e. In Gone with the Wind Scarlett O'Hara vowed, "Tomorrow is another day."

   f. The Exxon Company Board of Directors held their quarterly meeting yesterday.

   g. She robbed the bible from the hotel room.

   h. The bill of rights is composed of the first ten amendments to the constitution.

   i. Many persons enjoy back yard barbeques in the Summer.

   j. A realtor said the company had a $2.5 million-dollar investment in the land.

   k. The tremblor produced a flood in which the river crested at 25 feet above flood stage. Several cars and a Volkswagon van were swept down stream.

   l. The doctor took an x-ray and found the dog had swallowed a Yo-Yo.

   m. When police charged the man they found a cache of guns including a sawed off 12 guage shotgun, a 45 caliber pistol, and a .357 magnum.

   n. The farmer cried in anguish as he watched the funnel cloud destroy his barn.

   o. Despite warmer temperatures, much of the northeast remained in a deep freeze.

6. Space and time are precious commodities in the media, making it essential for editors to keep stories lean and make sure every word counts. Here are some redundant or wordy expressions you should look out for when editing copy:

acres of land
at the intersection of First and Elm streets
attitude of prejudice

close personal friend
10 different categories
due to the fact that
equally as

free gift
future plans
general consensus of opinion
general public

HIV virus
hot water heater
in the near future
in order to
is currently

located at
new developments in the case
past history/past experience

reason why
refer back/revert back
square feet of space
total destruction; totally demolished
whether or not

Edit the following sentences to eliminate redundancies and wordiness:

a. Two more names can be added to the list of students killed in school violence.

b. The City Council has approved funding to build a new municipal center for the city. It will be located downtown at the corner of Allen and Foster streets.

c. A hurricane totally demolished three summer homes on the bay.

d. Mayor Stephanie Thompson said she hoped to resolve the land-use dispute in the near future.

e. Past experience has shown that students need alternatives to alcohol-soaked events.

f. The Council is concerned about whether or not the new budget adequately allows for future plans.

g. The police chief nodded his head, acknowledging that there were finally some new developments in the Ramsey case.

h. The reason why the woman donated 10 acres of land to the city was because she did not think there was enough space devoted to parks.

i. The house has nearly 2,000 square feet of space and a new hot water heater.

j. Medications are improving the lives of people with the HIV virus. Some take a daily "cocktail" of several different drugs.

7. Transitions, like punctuation, serve as traffic signals. They signal shifts in thought and help guide the reader smoothly from idea to idea. Without transitions, stories read like facts strung together jerkily. Repetition of key words or phrases and the use of such transition words as *meanwhile* or *otherwise* are among transition techniques.

    a. Find a story in a newspaper or magazine that you think reads smoothly, and make a note of each transition technique used.

    b. Find a story in a newspaper or magazine in which you think transitions are lacking or ineffective. Suggest some words, phrases or reorganization that might smooth the flow of ideas.

8. Homonyms are words that are spelled and/or pronounced similarly but have very different meanings. And often, although your computer's spelling checker will catch typographic errors, stray keystrokes and outright misspellings, it may not alert you to misused or inappropriate words, including homonyms.
    Box 5.1 (on the next page) contains a list compiled by various journalists of some of the words that often come up in news writing and too often befuddle reporters and copy editors. It is by no means

comprehensive. You might develop your own list of words that trip you up and keep it handy when you're writing or editing. Even good spellers need to consult a dictionary or thesaurus frequently to ensure they are using words correctly and differentiating between shades of meaning.

These exercises will give you practice in choosing the correct words and ferreting out incorrect spellings and usage. Make corrections as needed. Watch for AP style errors, as well as word-usage problems.

a. Samuel Berger, President Clinton's national security advisor, said the Kosovo situation was entering a new faze.

b. The Republican Party picked Philadelphia as the sight for their national convention in 2000.

c. Many victims of the tornado remained in overcrowded temporary shelters.

d. The longtime Southern senator has changed his views on race relations, but he remains a died-in-the-wool conservative.

e. The proposal to develop a cul-de-sac at the end of Oak Lane illicited strong support from the neighborhood.

f. Embattled Microsoft chief Bill Gates denied he had distorted the truth in a videotaped deposition.

g. The United States had threatened eminent military action if Iraq did not comply with the U.N. resolutions.

h. Red Grooms' latest show is entitled "The Heroism of Modern Life."

i. The death toll from the hurricane rose to over 10,000.

j. More then 60 percent of Honduras' crops were destroyed in the storm.

k. Anybody with a computer and a modem could pour over the evidence against President Clinton.

Box 5.1 Homonyms and Other Word Problems

accept/except
adverse/averse
advice/advise
adviser (preferred spelling in news writing)
affect/effect
aid/aide
altar/alter
anxious/eager

bad/badly
biannual (twice a year; semiannual)
biennial (every two years)
bloc/block
bouillon/bullion
buses/busses

cancel/council/counsel/consul
canvas/canvass
carat/carrot/caret/karat
capital/capitol
cement/concrete
censored/censured
cite/sight/site
clamber/clamor
coarse/course
collide (implies both objects moving; otherwise, it's a crash)
complement/compliment
compose/comprise
convince/persuade
cord/chord
crowded (not overcrowded)

decent/descent/dissent
desert/dessert
desecrate/desiccate
discreet/discrete
disinterested/uninterested
dual/duel
dyeing/dying; died/dyed

elicit/illicit
elusive/illusive
embattled/beleaguered or besieged
emigrate/immigrate
eminent/imminent
ensure/insure
entitled/titled
epitaph/epithet
evoke/invoke

farther/further
faze/phase
flaunt/flout
fliers/flyers

gorilla/guerrilla
grisly/grizzly

hangar/hanger
hopefully (means full of hope; often misused to mean some outcome is hoped *for*)

imply/infer
incite/insight
its/it's

leave/let
lectern/podium
less/few
liable/libel

marshal/martial
may/might
mean/median/average
medal/metal
more than (not more *then;* usually preferred to "over" when referring to amounts or numbers)

nauseous/nauseated
naval/navel

oral/verbal (verbal can mean "oral" or "written")

palate/palette/pallet
passed/past
peal/peel
pedal/peddle
pore/pour
precede/proceed
prejudice/prejudiced
principal/principle

quiet/quite

rain/reign/rein
receipt/recipe
regardless (*not* irregardless, which would mean *not* regardless)

stationary/stationery

tenet/tenant
their/there/they're

unique (means "one of a kind"; something either is or is not, so there's no such thing as *very* unique)

weather/whether
who's/whose
you're/your

Skewed Sayings

dyed-in-the-wool (*not* died-in-the-wool)
couldn't care less (*not* could care less)
center on, or focus on (*not* center around)
while away the time (*not* wile)
take for granted (*not* granite)

l. The mayor described the public-private partnership as a very unique way to finance the downtown redevelopment project.

m. Sonny Bono collided with a tree while skiing.

n. Prison guards used black marks to censure the content of letters to the inmates.

o. Since we had only a verbal agreement, there is no written contract to tear up.

8. Find at least one example of a misused homonym or other word-usage mistake in your local newspaper or another medium. Explain the error and tell how you would correct it.

9. Circle the correct choice in each example.

   a. [Peels / Peals] of laughter rang out when the professor spilled coffee on his new tie.

   b. The [principal / principle] reason for tests is to check students' grasp of the material.

   c. Scaffolding has finally been removed from the refurbished Maryland [Capitol / Capital] in downtown Annapolis.

   d. The outnumbered House Democrats had hoped at least to [reign in/ rein in] the scope of the Clinton impeachment inquiry, but instead it became a wide-ranging investigation.

   e. Many people complain of boredom while [peddling / pedaling] away on a [stationery / stationary] bicycle to stay in shape.

   f. Paint fumes made the pregnant women [nauseous / nauseated].

   g. The mayor [implied / inferred] that it might take a tax increase to balance the municipal budget.

h. Police blocked off the [grisly / grizzly] accident scene, but not before at least one photographer shot a photo of the driver's body.

i. Chaos [reigned / reined] in the streets of the tiny nation's [capitol / capital] until the president imposed [martial / marshal] law on the city.

j. Honesty is one of the [tenants / tenets] of good journalism.

k. The victims included many women and children, [who's / whose] bodies were burned beyond recognition.

l. A one-[karat / caret / carat] diamond sparkled on her hand.

10. Strong, active verbs are the backbone of good writing. And this is perhaps even more evident in writing for the media. News, after all, involves activity; reporters tell stories about what's happening, what people are doing, how they are coping with situations.

    In each case, mark the verb as active (A) or passive (P). Then rewrite each of the passive-voice sentences to make it active.

    A   P

    ___ ___ The motion failed on a vote of 4-3.

    ___ ___ Council members were happy with the public's positive response.

    ___ ___ It was decided that a referendum would be placed on the fall ballot.

    ___ ___ The mayor left her purse on the bus.

    ___ ___ Smith was acquitted after only an hour of deliberation by the jury.

    ___ ___ The editor has left the office for the day.

    ___ ___ The homeless man had eaten nothing for two days.

A   P

___ ___ Police arrested Jayne Ambrosia for investigation of armed robbery.

___ ___ Patrick Malone was charged with impersonating a police officer.

___ ___ He didn't have change for a dollar.

___ ___ The hurricane has taken a big toll in lives and property damage.

___ ___ Money for a new stadium was taken out of the capital-improvements budget.

___ ___ The old woman was mugged by a robber in the park.

___ ___ In the contested election, victory is being claimed by the military leader.

___ ___ Unidentified gangsters blew Herbert "The Cat" Noble to bits Friday.

___ ___ Joelle majored in music at Oberlin before joining the Minneapolis Symphony.

___ ___ Parts of the law were declared unconstitutional by the courts.

11. Rewrite the following sentences to make the verbs active:

   a. The student was awakened by shouting and loud music.

   b. The mayor said he was not bothered by the council members' criticism.

   c. It's possible the professor was mistaken for a student by some of the alumni.

   d. Jen had been given a diamond ring by her maternal grandmother.

e. The home was destroyed by a fire that began in the kitchen. It was not noticed by neighbors until it was too late.

f. The game will be won by the team that can use strategy as well as brawn.

g. No decision on layoffs can be made by the company until more information about the economic outlook is obtained, according to the personnel director.

h. Shoppers were being charged inaccurately at the store until the scanner was repaired.

i. The car was dented by a deer, not a drunken driver, the owner testified.

j. It was decided by the City Council that traffic would be diverted from that street by signs.

k. The process of amniocentesis involves a needle being inserted through the mother's abdominal wall.

l. Neighbors were upset by the decision to rezone the corner lot for industrial development.

m. The book was written by a famous neurosurgeon who had suffered from depression.

n. American teen-agers have been spoiled by their affluent parents.

o. "Generation X" was a term used disparagingly by angry baby boomers.

p. Graffiti was spray-painted on the bridge by gang members, police say.

q. The cabin had deteriorated because it had not been visited by the family in years.

r. Officers said the school had been vandalized by some failing students.

s. A bomb threat was called in by someone just before the speech was to have begun.

t. The Wye accord was conditionally approved by the Israeli Cabinet on Wednesday.

12. Find an example of a sentence in your local newspaper that could be phrased in active, rather than passive, voice and rewrite it.

13. Find an example of a sentence in your local newspaper in which passive voice is appropriately used to place the emphasis on the action rather than the actor.

14. You probably learned as a child to avoid double negatives — that two negatives actually cancel each other out and result in a positive. But there are other ways that overuse of negative terms can trip up writers and editors. That's why you should try to keep these terms to a minimum. Rather than emphasizing what someone didn't do (as in City Council didn't pass the budget), try to substitute a stronger verb that tells what *did* happen: City Council rejected the budget.

    In the following passages, try to minimize the negative construction. But remember that quotations — sometimes deliberately muddled — should be handled with care. It is usually wise to consult with the writer before making changes in quotations or negative constructions.

    a. It's not too late to write your representative and urge him or her not to vote for the bill, which would not protect wetlands in the area.

    b. "I'm not saying I don't disagree with the governor," the senator said at a press conference.

    c. Brown denied that he had not voted in the last three presidential elections.

    d. It's often not the case that students don't understand the assignment when they botch it.

    e. The controversial bill would require tavern owners to prove they did not fail to ask for identification from underage drinkers.

    f. The Council decided not to vote yet on the ordinance not to remove the traffic barriers.

15. Find an example of a confusing or unnecessary negative construction in a headline, photo caption or article in your local newspaper or another publication. How would you reword it?

16. Clichés, jargon and slang creep into media writing because of time pressure, lack of clear thinking or overzealous attempts to make writing sound conversational. Your job, as an editor, is to be vigilant for these flaws and eliminate them.

    Find an example of a cliché, jargon or slang expression in a headline, caption or story in your local newspaper or another publication. Suggest a possible rewording.

17. Rewrite each of the following passages to eliminate the cliché, jargon, slang or stilted language. (*Note:* Some of the following exercises have been adapted from *The Word: An Associated Press Guide to Good News Writing*, Rene J. Cappon, NY: 1982.)

    a. Los Angeles area residential real estate holdings ...

    b. ... so it can afford to re-equip its fleet with new, fuel-efficient jets.

    c. The situation poses a danger to the public because of the tendency of persons on probation to commit more crimes.

    d. The two leaders decided to set up a consultative mechanism, in which diplomats from both sides would meet regularly on specific issues.

    e. The board of directors, after hours of wrangling, lowered the boom on Taylor, the corporation's third top honcho to get the ax in two years.

    f. The late shah of Iran, who got kicked out of the country, was forced into wandering when country after country sent him packing.

    g. It's late in the game for legislative reform, but the moment of truth has finally arrived.

    h. The coach said everyone on the team gave 110 percent, and they finally got the monkey off their back, beating Green Bay for the first time in five gridiron battles.

i. He was a front-runner in a crowded field, but he stumbled in a crucial primary with a dark horse closing fast, so it appears the convention will go down to the wire.

j. Torrential rains failed to dampen the spirits of a crowd that turned out for the Centennial Parade.

18. Metaphors and similes can energize news writing. They can help the reader envision or understand the unfamiliar by drawing parallels with something familiar or more concrete. But, they also can be overdone. Some metaphorical expressions have been so overused that they've become stale and drag down rather than add vitality to a piece of writing. You should eliminate protracted, mixed and mismatched metaphors. Find an example of a skillfully used metaphor in a newspaper, magazine or book. Explain why you think the expression works well.

19. Rewrite each passage to eliminate clumsy metaphors.

a. The scandal is the latest storm to engulf the president, but it is just the latest chapter in a long series of tangled events.

b. The challenger arrived in Kent, Ohio, this morning as he continued his drive to throw sand into the motor of the incumbent's juggernaut.

c. His neighborhood, nestled between the foothills and the river, remains a womb of friends, family and fellow Hispanics, but it has suffered from police layoffs, an increase in burglaries and the destruction or abandonment of many homes.

d. Smith, an avid sailor, has been at the helm of his company five years, and during that time has steered it past many shoals.
   The worst squall he faced was a bitter proxy fight, but he weathered it and the seas have been calm ever since.
   In fact, the only one who makes waves now is Smith himself.

e. Home-mortgage interest rates sprouted fresh skids today.

f. His eyebrows furrowed in a tempestuous stare.

20. Quotations add authenticity, as well as enliven stories. Because they are presented as the speaker's exact words, the editor must treat them with respect. Be sure you don't alter quotations so their meaning is distorted, and be sure that in trimming a story with opposing viewpoints that you don't cut one side's arguments so the story becomes unbalanced. Speaking of balance, remember that *said* is the best, most neutral attribution word. Avoid "loaded" words such as *claimed*. Usually, it's best for the attribution to follow the quotation, but there are exceptions. Also, avoid unnecessary repetition between the paraphrased "setup" and the quotation itself. And finally, resist the temptation to put quotation marks around paraphrased material. Just because the word *said* appears, you can't assume it's a direct quote.

Edit the following passages to eliminate unnecessary repetition, position attribution appropriately or paraphrase to eliminate unnecessary and/or partial quotes:

a. Brady said he accepted the position because it would be a "challenge."

b. The senator said that "during this period of time, which covered six years, this subcommittee held a total of only six days of hearings."

c. Two of United's chief competitors, Delta Airlines and American Airlines, immediately said they would match the reduced fares.
   "We have and always will remain competitive. Anything we can do to remain competitive we will do," John Rodgers, a Delta spokesman in Atlanta, said.
   "It's fair to say that we will be there with a program of our own. We simply must and will be competitive," American Airlines spokesman Al Becker noted.

d. The mayor described the parking garage as a "key" element of the downtown redevelopment plan.

e. "There may be occasions, crimes, when the death penalty appears justified. At least many people think so. I have sometimes leaned that way myself, but to my mind, large problems always remain," he said.

f. "I can't go home, I live too far away. I live in South Carolina and it's just too far. It annoys me that I would have to have this break just so some people who live close can have a chance to go home," sophomore Kassandra Tucker said.

g. "Self-defense does not make a person more violent. Instead, it provides a more confident understanding of your options and capabilities," Frank Smith, manager of Wings Self-Defense Center, stated.

h. Why is it so hard for original music to thrive in this town? Miller says, "To put it harshly, people are sheep and will let themselves be led by TV, radio and advertising down the path of least resistance instead of forming their own opinions."

i. "The Air Force has higher social and academic standards than is required of other students. Cadets in the Air Force ROTC program are expected to act like officers. A proper attitude, appearance and manners are expected at all times," Matthew Schneider, junior—telecommunications, a cadet third class in the Air Force ROTC, said.

j. Some students agree that alcohol has a major impact on them. "Alcohol has definitely affected my grades. I think I would have done better if I didn't drink," Jayne Miller, 21, junior—computer engineering, said.

21. Well-structured sentences sing; improperly structured sentences clunk. As an editor, you need to watch for parallel construction, dangling or misplaced modifiers, sentence fragments and non sequiturs that can bog down a story or leave readers scratching their heads wondering what the writer really meant.
    Edit the following sentences to make them read more smoothly.

    a. Although Glenn's first launch was not covered by so many reporters, which is not to say it went unnoticed.

    b. Johnson said he admired Martha Stearns for her intelligence, energy, and because she is a good leader.

    c. First, he walked in, then he smiled, then he says "Hello."

    d. Sam enjoyed researching a topic, conducting interviews and then to write up his findings.

    e. The politician was both informed about the legislation and cared about the people it would help.

    f. The new fall break is not a University holiday, meaning no classes will be scheduled, but faculty and staff are still required to come to work the two days students have off.

    g. Approved in September by the Board of Trustees, 30 core faculty members, plus 25 new faculty members at other campuses are projected for the new School of Information Sciences and Technology.

    h. Fund-raising dancers energized by the kids they sponsor, support and morale from their organization and the mass amounts of food, which are donated by campus eateries.

i. Living in a college town with thousands of rental properties, it should not be startling that bitter tenant-landlord disputes occur.

j. However, sometimes blindness is inevitable such was the case for Kevin Schlessinger.

k. Hect listed the pros of military life as job security, professionalism, knowing what to do every day, and traveling. His cons were being away from family and friends and set ranges of pay.

l. A mother of three, Meskin was born in Wichita Falls, Texas, but moved to Green Bay, Wis., at age 9.

m. Some easy approaches to handling stress are positive thinking, setting realistic goals, more laughter, accepting what cannot be changed, and "nowness," or living in the present.

n. Fines for expired meters, wrong area parking and parking in a handicapped space were also increased last semester.

o. By prioritizing, it becomes clear that a Friday morning essay exam is more important than a Thursday night at the bar, and squabbling with a roommate is not World War III.

PART 2

Inside the Story

CHAPTER 6

News close to home: Editing local stories and community news

Probably no other part of the news elicits more reader response than local stories. And because the people and places in these stories are so familiar, readers may delight in pointing out inaccuracies in spellings and facts. That's why copy editors must be especially vigilant about accuracy and fairness in these articles.

Too often, obituaries in particular do not get the attention they deserve. An obituary is a tribute to the subject, whose name might otherwise never have been in the newspaper. And, although it's much shorter and less spectacular than the multipart Sunday project story, an obituary actually may have a much longer "shelf life," with copies mailed to out-of-town loved ones and saved for years in family Bibles.

Another role of the editor may be to localize a national story — to find out whether a particular problem or trend exists closer to home and, if so, how it's affecting residents. Localizing may be a matter of simply finding some information and inserting a few sentences into a wire story. Or, a local sidebar or related story might be appropriate. In any case, coordination between local and wire editors is essential in copy editing, page design and headline writing. Such coordination emphasizes the local relevance and avoids both duplication and conflicts in information.

Exercises

1. Take a look at several local articles in a local newspaper. Make a note of any editing errors you find and show how you would improve the copy.

2. Find a national or international story in a newspaper, and describe how you could localize it for a newspaper in your community. Explain, for example, where you would insert local details. Or you could suggest a sidebar or a complete local story.

3. Edit the following stories according to your professor's instructions, checking the "usual suspects": style, grammar, punctuation, accuracy and objectivity. Use the map and city directory in the appendix to check names and locations. Make a note of any missing or confusing information you would need to check out with the writer.

   a. School board

   The Spring Valley Board of Education cleared up some parent's misconceptions about a recent impromptu pep rally at the high school and elected officers at it's regular meeting Monday night at 7:00 PM at Kennedy High School.

53

Robert Bannister addressed the concerns of parents regarding a pep rally that took place in the high school on November 20. About 300 students left their classes on that day and did a "snake dance" through the halls of the building. The dancers eventually made they're way to the gymnasium where a pep rally ensued in support of the football team.

Several students were suspended for vandalism that occurred during the pep rally, but some say that the Administration got the wrong students. Many parents argue the administration caught good kids taking part in a harmless school spirit activity.

"I just think the school really overreacted," said parent John McNichols who's fifteen-year-old son, Scott attends Kennedy. "It's so unfair to ruin the records of some really decent kids."

"Suspensions are appropriate for those kinds of defiance and vandalism", Banister said defending the school administrators decision.

Some college applications ask if a student was ever suspended and parents are worried that this suspension for what they see as a trivial matter could jeopardize their children's future.

The school board agreed that the appropriate disciplines were handed down and they will assist any student that desires it in explaining the reason why they were suspended on college applicaitons.

Before this fairly heated discussion between Bannister, board members, and parents, the board elected their officers for next year. Carla Buchanan was re-elected President by a unanimous vote. Cynthia Potter stepped down as Vice-President after 5 years, and was replaced by Marc Sherrill.

The Spring Valley School Board meets on the second and fourth Tuesday of every month, accept in Dec., when they meet on the first and third. The meetings are rotated between the various elementary, secondary, and high schools throughout the District.

b. Hancock obit

    Kelly Hancock, 86 a resident of the Paradise residential care center, died Tuesday at the home.

    She was born December 20, 1914 in Yuma, Arizona, a daughter of the late Richard and Hannah O'Keeffe. She married Don C. Hancock, who died Nov. 15, 1985.

    A cook for the Spring Valley School District for 20 years before retiring in 1980, she and her family moved to the area when she was ten years old.

    She was a long-time member and a past elder of the First Presbyterian Church and a member of the adult Sunday School class there, she also taught children's Sunday School classes for many years. She also was a 50 year member and past matron of the local chapter Order of the Eastern Star, Secretary of the chapter for five years, and a member of the Spring Creek Fire company Lady's Auxiliary.

    She is survived by a daughter, Agnes Irene Johnson of Spring Valley, three sons, John of Norfolk, VA, Thomas of Cleveland and Michael of Kenosha, Wisc, two sisters, May Lewis and Betsy Byars, both of Denver, 15 grandchildren, two stepgrandchildren, 10 great-grandchildren and one great-great grandchild.

    Visitation will be from 2-4 PM and from 7-9 PM at the McCoy Funeral Home, 102 East Elm Street.

    Funeral will be at 10 AM Saturday at the First Presbyterian Church with Reverend Myrna Malloy officiating. Her body will be cremated and the ashes will be scattered in the Rocky mountains she loved to hike in according to family members.

    Memorial contributions in lieu of flowers may be made to the First Presbyterian Church Building Fund, the Sierra Club, or the American Cancer Society.

-30-

c. United Way

The United Way kicked off an ambitious campaign Monday announcing it's goal of $1,600,000 during a catered luncheon of shrimp and prime rib attended by the Mayor and other city and county leaders.

Pledge cards will be received by participating area companies and businesses in the next couple of weeks, according to this year's chairman Asa Gardner.

"We want to emphasize that the United Way truly is a way for our community to be united in helping others", Gardner stated during the luncheon at which team captains were announced as well as this year's goal.

Gardener reminded donors that they can choose the specific organizations they want to contribute their money to or they can donate to the United Way at large, noting that last year's goal was exceeded by reaching a record $1,500,050, hence the increased goal for this year.

The harsh winter last year took it's toll on some United Way concerns including the battered womens' shelter which was filled to capacity on some frigid nights and had to turn away many women and children, said Gardner, who claimed that the local United Way chapter only uses about five per cent of its funds for administration.

Everyone is urged to give generously to this important charitable effort that does so much in our community. For more information call 555-5555 and ask to speak to Candy.

-30-

d. Library

A 3-dimensional model of the proposed new library building at Alan and Forest Streets can be seen on display at the Municipal Building downtown this week. The model was presented to the city's Library Building Committee at their monthly meeting Tuesday by the architect James Gantt & Associates.

The model includes the surrounding existing buildings like the Municipal Building, the downtown Days Inn, the Courthouse, and the Art Museum. The new library is to be named in honor of Katy Langston a long-time patron of the library who remembered it in her will by bequeathing $1,000,000 to the building fund.

"I am delighted that we have reached this major mile stone in bringing a long overdue improvement to the downtown not to mention providing some much needed space for our books and other materials. We look forward to being able to serve our patrons more effectively," said Marla Perkins the chief librarian. "This is a key part of revitalizing our downtown area as a cultural as well as commercial center".

Other Committee members said they did not find any serious faults with the architect's model but they will have some suggestions for refining some aspects of it. Floor plans are also on display as part of the model.

Perkins says the committee welcomes ideas and written comments from the general public and she hopes many citizens will take advantage of the opportunity and attend a number of meetings that will be held in the next two weeks to present their comments. The first of those meetings will be held at noon Friday.

The City Council also invites comments from the public during the public hearing at their next meeting at 7:00 PM Monday night.

-30-

e. Rescue

A ten-year-old boy was trapped in a 12-inch wide drainage pipe for 4 hours Wednesday before volunteer firefighters came to the rescue.

Tom Larkin was unharmed. He was treated and released at Hope Memorial Hospital, possibly suffering from the chilly temperature.

"I'm OK. It was pretty dark and scary in there and pretty cold too but I'm fine now. All I have is some bruises," said the boy this morning.

Around 12 noon, Tom was playing soccer with some friends at Sunset Park when he tried to climb through the 200-foot-long pipe to retrieve the ball.

"He said I can crawl through there. I know where the other side is," according to Myles Thompson, also 10 and one of Tom's friends. Myles said that he and the other friends told Tom they would go get help if he did get stuck in the pipe.

Tom got about halfway through before he couldn't go any further.

"He kept yelling, 'I'm tired. I can't go any further,' said another friend, Shawn Freeman, 11. "We could hear him crying".

The boys ran to a nearby convenience store to use the phone and call the police then returned to the pipe and yelled to Tom that help was on the way.

Larry Larkin, Tom's father, seemed amazed that his son would attempt such a feat. "He's not very adventurous. He's usually really timid, especially about heights and small spaces," Larkin sighed shaking his head.

Larkin and about 50 other people watched as rescue workers dug a six-foot-square hole to reach the pipe where Tom was stuck. The rescue workers dug the hole in a pipe joint and they monitored the air in the pipe to insure that Tom was getting enough oxygen. They were talking to him the whole time as they dug the hole and inserted a metal trench box to keep the hole from collapsing.

The five firefighters who responded to the scene attempted several different techniques to rescue Tom, who wasn't actually stuck but told them that after rolling over and crawling about 100 feet on his stomach that he was too exhausted to continue.

"I didn't have much room in there," he said later, "I had to basically stay in one position the whole four hours."

The firefighters used a vice-like tool and cut into the pipe about 10 feet from where Tom was laying on his stomach. Steven Kappelli, the smallest of the firemen who at 5 feet 7 and 135 pounds is only slightly larger than Tom himself, entered the small opening to help Tom.

Just after 4:00 PM Tom was able to crawl 10 feet and was carried up a ladder by the waiting firefighters.

"He was shivering. We were obviously concerned about hypothermia because it was getting very cold in the afternoon and he wasn't dressed warmly. But we were relieved that he had no apparent injuries," said Fire Chief Robert Henry.

The pipes in Sunset Park mainly drain water from the playing fields and into culverts nearby. There was no water in the pipes on Wednesday when Tom crawled inside.

The county Parks and Recreation Department plans to study the drainage system at all the county parks to determine whether they can prevent a similar incident from occurring, a spokesman said. Henry said he couldn't remember any previous incident of a child being caught in one of the pipes.

For his part, Tom won't be chasing any more balls into drainage pipes. "I learned my lesson," he grinned sheepishly.

-30-

f. Shooting

Linda McBee was shot Friday on her way to see her mother before work just after boarding the Route S bus at the corner of Oak and Shasta.

Right after she found a seat a gunman tried to take the 25-year-old woman's purse and her diamond engagement ring. She screamed and a shot was fired.

The bullet from a 9 mm handgun struck McBee in her chest. It exited her body and went through the side of the bus which was in front of a school and luckily for McBee just down the street from Hope Memorial Hospital

As the gunman fled from the bus after failing to get either the purse or the ring, passengers rushed to McBee's aid. She was taken to the hospital and after undergoing several hours of surgery was listed in critical but stable condition last night.

The gunman was chased by several of the witnesses, but they lost him on Shasta. But police quickly arrived on the scene and soon found a suspect hiding in a nearby alley.

Earle Hagman, 22 was arrested without incident for attempted murder, robbery and weapons-related charges.

McBee's family and friends gathered at the hospital. They described her as a loving, caring woman who just happened to be in the wrong place at the wrong time. A few months ago, she became engaged to be married.

"Everyone is just distraught. She is the sweetest girl, always doing something to help other people. She was on that particular bus because she was going to do an errand for her sick mother on the way to work," her grandmother, Bessie Simms said.

Transit officials say that they can't recall the last time a bus rider was shot.

-30-

g. Meltdown

Despite the melting of the recent heavy snow and the ensuing threat of flooding, several counties remain under drought emergencies.

Mike Abrams, forecaster at the local National Weather Service office said flooding may become a problem in the next few days as warm air and rain move into the area.

He said there's more than two inches of water in the snow and ice pack on the ground now, and if all that melts and is combined with over an inch of rain, there could be some flooding.

People who live in low-lying, flood-prone areas should watch the water levels, advises the county's emergency management coordinator.

The problem is that not much of the snow and rain is getting down to the water table, Abrams said. Frozen ground and storm drains are keeping the moisture from sinking into the ground where it could do some good, instead water is pooling in low-lying areas and running into creeks and streams, raising the danger of flooding, he adds.

Emily and Randy Hayes own a farm in a low valley along Spring Creek. Ironically, they are looking out for flood warnings even while trying to limit their water usage.

"We're taking shorter showers, and we haven't washed the truck in weeks," Emily said. "Heck, we're not even flushing the toilet every time," she laughed.

East of Spring Valley, tree limbs were blown down and power was disrupted by heavy winds yesterday, gusting to 70 mph. A funnel cloud touched down in neighboring Lee County, destroying a barn and a house that fortunately was unoccupied.

In nearby Jonesville a motorist slid on an icy patch on a bridge and his car was swept into Deer Creek. The motorist, Andrew Stevens, was rescued by volunteer firefighters and transported to Hope Memorial Hospital where he was reported in serious condition being treated for hypothermia.

-30-

CHAPTER 7

News from Afar: Editing Wire Stories

Sometimes the wire editor has the most fascinating job in the newsroom. Also the most nerve-wracking. This person has, at his or her fingertips, the breaking stories of the day from all over the world. Comedians have quipped that it's interesting that just enough news happens every day to fill up all the newspapers of the world. Wire editors know better. Way more happens. Determining what's most interesting, useful and relevant to that paper's audience is a major part of the wire editor's responsibilities. Some days, it seems that stories are constantly breaking and being updated right through deadline. Other days, the wires are "dead," and the news editor may be pleading with the city desk editor to come up with a lead story.

The job becomes even more challenging for editors at papers that subscribe to more than one wire service: They must choose which version of a story is most complete, perhaps combining information from a supplemental service or other wire story.

As the wires are sorted and stories doled out to the various desks, other copy editors are trimming and/or combining versions, localizing and writing headlines on these stories. Some desks handle only wire copy, while another desk edits local stories; in other newsrooms, these responsibilities are combined on one "universal" news desk.

When editing wire copy, you need a sense of history and good grasp of the major news events occurring around the world. But you also should be alert to opportunities for local spin-offs: inserts, sidebars and related stories. The following exercises are designed to give you practice in those skills.

Exercises

1. Make a list of the top 10 international, national and state/regional stories in the news. For each of these, write a brief summary of the latest major developments.

2. Skim through your local newspaper and make a note of all the wire services credited for stories, photos and graphics.

3. Go to the library and choose several newspapers from different areas of the nation to examine. Find the same national or world story reported by different wire services in these papers. Does one paper display the story more prominently on the page with a bigger headline? Is one paper's version significantly longer than another's? Make a list of facts included in one story but missing from another. Are there any discrepancies between the different wire services' accounts? Compare the leads. Does one wire service use a summary lead and another take a different approach? Which do you find more appropriate?

4. Find a national story that could be localized for your area, and explain how this could be done. If you were a copy editor on deadline and needed to insert a bit of local information in this story, what resources could you use?

5. Combine the following two stories into one about 20 inches long (or the length specified by your instructor), and change the credit to "Wire Services." Make a note of any discrepancies and/or style differences you find. Also, create either a reaction sidebar or a sidebar on the apparent tie-in with Veterans/ Remembrance Day, of 10 to 12 inches. Try not to include too much duplication from the main story.

SNIPER A

BY CAROLYN THOMPSON
THE ASSOCIATED PRESS

AMHERST, N.Y. — A sniper killed a doctor who performs abortions, firing through the physician's kitchen window — the first fatality among five sniper attacks on upstate New York or Canadian abortion providers in the last four years.

Dr. Barnett Slepian, 51, a target of anti-abortion protesters since the 1980s, was gunned down Friday night. The killing came days after authorities warned abortion providers in the region about possible violence because the four earlier attacks happened within a few weeks of Nov. 11, Veterans Day.

"There's some type of connection on the date. We don't know what it is," Inspector David Bowen of the Hamilton-Wentworth (Ont.) police said Saturday.

Bowen is part of a Canadian-American task force that has investigated the shootings since November 1997. Task force spokesman Keith McCaskill said the shooter or shooters had not contacted authorities following any of the attacks.

Slepian's wife told police the shooting happened minutes after the couple returned home from synagogue. The Slepians' four sons, ages 7 to 15, also were home at the time.

Before Slepian, three Canadian doctors and a doctor near Rochester, N.Y., were shot and wounded since 1994. In each case, the doctors were fired upon with a high-powered rifle through windows in their homes. Canadian and American authorities issued safety tips to doctors on Tuesday.

"They were told to stay away from windows that weren't covered with curtains or blinds and to be aware of their surroundings and anything suspicious at their clinics," said Frank Olesko, Amherst's assistant police chief.

Slepian's killer shot through a winder with raised blinds from behind a backyard fence. A helicopter search was fruitless. The gunman remained at large Saturday.

On a list of doctors who perform abortions, clinic workers and others compiled posted on a Web site, Slepian's name had a line through it. The list names abortion providers it says are working, wounded or have been killed.

The Web site, which has rantings against homosexuality and the government, includes photos of aborted fetuses and has links to the Army of God. Letters signed by the shadowy Army of God claimed responsibility for the 1997 bombings of a gay bar in Atlanta and an abortion clinic, and the fatal Birmingham abortion clinic bombing.

Abortion supporters and foes alike condemned the attack.

"For anyone to take it upon himself to be judge, jury and executioner is nothing but sheer evil," said Karen Swallow Prior, formerly of the anti-abortion group Operation Rescue and now the Right-to-Life Party candidate for lieutenant governor.

Gov. George Pataki said the killer should face the death penalty: "It's beyond a tragedy — it's really an act of terrorism and, in my mind, a cold-blooded assassination."

Anti-abortion protesters had targeted Slepian before. Activists claimed victory when Slepian temporarily closed his Amherst office in 1992 during a protest by Operation Rescue in the Buffalo area.

Slepian closed the office to avoid inconveniencing other doctors in his building, he said at the time, promising to continue performing abortions at a clinic in Buffalo.

"He was one of the few physicians in this area with the integrity to stand up for what he believed in," said Marilynn Buckham of HYN Womenservices, a Buffalo clinic. "Those who picket the doctors and clinic — the anti-choice extremists — contribute to this environment of hate and hostility."

Slepian had promised not to let frequent confrontations with protesters deter him.

"He said, 'They're not going to scare me. They're not going to threaten me,'" said Harvey Rogers, a lawyer who represented Slepian after the doctor faced charges following a 1988 clash with protester in front of his home.

-30-

SNIPER B

BY JIM YARDLEY AND DAVID ROHDE
THE NEW YORK TIMES

AMHERST, N.Y., Oct. 24 – Dr. Barnett Slepian, an obstetrician with a practice in this Buffalo suburb, returned home from synagogue Friday night with his wife, Lynn, and greeted his four sons. Then he stepped into his kitchen, where a sniper's bullet crashed through a back window and struck him in the chest, the police said.

He fell to the floor, calling for help, and died within two hours.

Dr. Slepian was one of three doctors who provide abortions in the Buffalo area, and investigators said his killing was the most deadly evidence yet of a pattern of anti-abortion sniper shootings in Canada and western New York.

Earlier in the week, the F.B.I. joined a Canadian law enforcement task force trying to solve four sniper attacks against abortion doctors dating back to 1994. Canadian officials said the shootings appeared to be connected and warned of "a high probability that these attacks will continue."

The shooting of Dr. Slepian, 51, apparently fulfilled this prophecy. He is the third abortion doctor killed in the United States since 1993. He had endured years of picketing and harassment, apparently moving his family into a new home in a quiet, affluent subdivision two years ago in hopes of avoiding protesters.

The four other shootings — three in Canada and one in Rochester — each occurred within a few weeks of Nov. 11, or Veterans Day, known as Remembrance Day in Canada. Carla Eckhardt of the Washington-based National Abortion Federation, an abortion-rights organization, said earlier in the week that some Canadian anti-abortion activists call the holiday "Remember the Unborn Children Day."

In each of the attacks, the snipers used a high-powered rifle, firing through a window of the doctors' homes. Investigators are looking at the possibility that the same gunman is responsible for all the shootings.

President Clinton said today that he was "outraged" by Dr. Slepian's slaying and that the Justice Department was working with the local authorities to track down his killer.

Gov. George E. Pataki said the killer should face the death penalty.

"It's beyond tragedy — it's really an act of terrorism and, in my mind, a cold-blooded assassination," Mr. Pataki said today in Buffalo.

Susan Ward, a spokeswoman for Buffalo GYN Women's Services, the private clinic where Dr. Slepian performed abortions, said the National Abortion Federal had faxed a warning to the clinic Friday morning reminding them about the four-year pattern of attacks. Ms. Ward said the fax was sent to Dr. Slepian at his private office in Amherst.

"He was aware of the threat," she said today. "Around this time of year, there had been shootings."

The Rev. Flip Benham, national director for the anti-abortion group Operation Rescue, issued a statement today that neither condoned nor condemned the killing. Mr. Benham traced "the spirit of murder" to the Roe v. Wade decision that legalized abortion in 1973. "We have shed the blood of the innocent in the womb, and we are now reaping it in the streets," he said.

Gloria Feldt, president of the Planned Parenthood Federation of America, which represents more than 400 abortion clinics across the nation, described the killing as "evil terrorism." She criticized police agencies in the Buffalo area for failing to protect Dr. Slepian.

"Law enforcement had been notified that a threat had been issued against all the providers of abortion services in northern New York and Canada," she said today at a Manhattan news conference.

The gunman who shot Dr. Slepian apparently hid in a strip of woods behind his house, then fired a single shot from a high-powered rifle, investigators said. Local police officers, F.B.I. agents and Canadian investigators searched the woods today, but the identity and whereabouts of the suspect remained unknown.

The Slepians lived in Roxbury Park, an affluent Amherst subdivision of two-story Tudor-style homes. The police had cordoned off the family's home with crime scene tape. Several teen-age friends of Dr. Slepian's sons gathered today outside the house, including Eric Balsom, 13, who said he spoke with the youngest son, Philip, 7, early this morning.

"He's asking: 'Where's my Dad? Is he going to come back?'" Eric said.

David Neale, 14, said the Slepians moved from a nearby house two years ago to avoid protesters. "It was because he was an abortion doctor," David said.

Dr. Shalom Press, another Amherst abortion provider who had known Dr. Slepian for years, said, "He believed women had the right to have an abortion, and he followed his conscience."

The slaying comes six years after anti-abortion protesters descended on Buffalo. In April 1982, the city was the setting for a coordinated series of "Spring of

Life" protests led by members of the anti-abortion group Operation Rescue. Nearly 200 protesters were arrested during one demonstration, and abortion-rights groups held counterprotests. The police said that Dr. Slepian was one of the doctors singled out by anti-abortion picketers.

Dr. Slepian fully understood the risks he took. In April 1993, one month after the shooting death of a Pensacola, Fla., abortion provider, Dr. David Gunn, Dr. Slepian spoke to a reporter about the vulnerability of doctors who provide abortions. "It probably hits home a little bit because it could have been me," Dr. Slepian told the Buffalo News. "For years I've felt, and I still feel, it could happen to me or to someone around me."

And in 1995, after a Roman Catholic bishop had picketed outside his office, he told The News: "When you're using words like 'kill' and 'murder,' that's where it can lead. If the rosary-holding churchgoers and the Bishop don't think that's true, they're fooling themselves."

In 1988, Dr. Slepian had clashed with anti-abortion protesters outside his home. Protesters had taunted him during the Jewish holiday of Hanukkah, calling him a "murderer."

One protester later said that Dr. Slepian had attacked him with a baseball bat, and Dr. Slepian was charged with felony assault. The charge was later reduced to a misdemeanor and he was fined $400 for damaging the protester's vehicle.

Dr. Slepian divided his practice between the clinic in Buffalo and his private office in Amherst. Ms. Ward, the clinic spokeswoman, said he had worked at that and other clinics for 15 years. "He has been harassed right in front of his house," she said. "His children have been harassed."

A woman from Attica, N.Y., who identified herself only as Susan, stood outside his Amherst office today weeping. She said he had delivered her niece and her daughter and that he kept a photo album of the hundreds of babies he had delivered.

"To me, he was about babies, not abortion," Susan said. She said she went to him every three months for the past four years for treatment of cervical cancer. "I feel he saved my life. I feel he is like a member of my family."

The four shootings that preceded Dr. Slepian's death began on Nov. 8, 1994, when a doctor in Vancouver, British Columbia, was struck in the leg by a bullet fired into his home, Canadian authorities said earlier in the week. The next year, on Nov. 10, a physician in the province of Ontario was shot in the right elbow through his den window. Last year, on Oct. 28, a gunshot was fired at a doctor in his home near Rochester. The shot missed him, but the doctor was wounded by flying debris from the bullet. Two weeks later, a doctor in Winnipeg, Manitoba, was shot in his right shoulder as he stood in the rear of his house.

-30-

6. Combine the following two stories into one about 15 inches long (or a length specified by your instructor), and change the credit to "Wire Services." Make a note of any discrepancies and/or style differences you find.

CULT A

BY CHARLIE BRENNAN
DENVER ROCKY MOUNTAIN NEWS STAFF WRITER

Israel on Monday ordered 11 members of a Denver-based doomsday cult deported and three others held for further investigation.

Authorities suspect John Bayles of Denver, Terry Smith of Eagle and Eric Malesic of Westminster plotted to start a gunfight with police in Jerusalem, an incident the trio believed would trigger the Second Coming of Jesus Christ and a biblical apocalypse.

They denied the allegation Monday.

"I am not here to hurt anybody," Bayles told magistrate Nira Diskin. Diskin ordered the trio held for 48 hours so police could complete their investigation.

Bayles, Smith, Malesic and 11 others were arrested Sunday after police raided two homes in the western suburbs of Jerusalem.

The judge ordered the others, including six children, deported. They have 72 hours to appeal.

All 14 are followers of Monte Kim Miller, a 44-year-old Denver man who leads the apocalyptic sect Concerned Christians.

Miller has predicted that he will die on the streets of Jerusalem next December, shortly before Christ's Second Coming and the end of the world.

The charismatic preacher and more than 70 followers disappeared from Colorado in October — two months before, according to Miller, Denver was to be destroyed.

Miller is not among those arrested, and his whereabouts remain a mystery to officials. Many of his followers are believed to be in Mexico.

Other arrests in Israel are possible. Kurt and Keith Landaas of Yellow Jacket are believed to be in the country, as are Gary and Cheryl Schmidt and their two children. Their names are on the lease of abandoned apartments found several weeks ago in Jerusalem.

Norm Smith of Denver, the father of Terry Smith, worries whether Miller will be held accountable for any charges or allegations against his followers.

"Where's Kim Miller?" he asked. "Obviously, he made sure he wasn't going to be around, so that he wouldn't get hurt. He'll probably abscond, grow a beard, and start all over again."

Still, should any of the allegations against his son and others be proved, Norm Smith was offering no excuses for his child.

"That's devastating," he said, of the reported plot to provoke Israeli police into an incendiary gun battle. "He was not raised that way, at all."

U.S. State Department workers visited with the three women and six children who were swept up in the raids but were not permitted to see the five men — including Bayles, Malesic and Smith — who are being held.

A spokeswomen said the women and children were in good condition. They are are being held at the staff dormitory of the Israeli border police headquarters.

Deportation of the women and children was not yet under way at 1 a.m. today Israel time. A schedule for the deportation had not been announced.

Israeli law allows 72 hours for foreigners to appeal a deportation order.

The Denver cultists were arrested by a newly formed Israeli task force consisting of police, agents of the domestic Shin Bet security service and the Mossad spy agency.

Police won't disclose evidence about those arrested. An Israeli law enforcement source said much of the impetus for the raid came from intelligence concerning the Concerned Christians' beliefs, relayed by U.S. authorities — rather than crimes committed in Israel.

First Sgt. Ilan Granot told the court that officials worried that Bayles might try to take his own life, and that he was being watched closely.

"I don't feel I pose a threat to anybody," Bayles said.

Interior Minister Eli Suissa suggested that the suspects may have planned to commit suicide and not harm anyone else.

"We don't want such people here, not that we are against tourists coming. But they shouldn't do things we don't want them to," Suissa said on Israel army radio.

Kim Loepp of Aurora found out for sure that her brother, 21-year-old David Campbell, was in Israel when she glimpsed him being arrested there on television.

"Nobody told me he was in the cult until I saw it on the news," said Loepp, 25. "I saw his picture on TV last night. I was crying."

Loepp said Campbell was recruited into Concerned Christians by his neighbors in Littleton, Tony and Rhonda "Ronnie" Luzano.

"Tony and Ronnie, they live next door to my stepdad," said Loepp. "They tried getting us involved with it, like, two years ago. But, I just thought she was crazy."

She believes her stepbrother was pulled into the group because he was lonely.

"He went to work, he came home, and just kind of kicked it, by himself. He'd drink. He'd party. He never acted like he was totally into religion. This guy, Miller, twisted his brain something bad."

Mark Roggeman, a Denver police officer who tracks Miller's group in his spare time, said Sunday's arrest could shake Miller's group to its foundation.

"I want to see is what kind of two-step Kim is going to do," said Roggeman. "One thing about a biblical prophet, they have to be 100 percent correct 100 percent of the time, or they're not from God. These people probably thought they were in a safe environment."

-30-

CULT B

BY PEGGY LOWE, KEVIN SIMPSON AND VIRGINIA CULVER
DENVER POST STAFF WRITERS

Jan. 5 – Israel took swift and severe action against members of a Denver apocalyptic cult Monday, ordering deportation for the women and children while jailing three men for plotting violence at Jerusalem's holy sites.

A day after an 100-officer-strong raid on two suburban homes where 14 members of Concerned Christians were living, the three Colorado men appeared in court and were ordered held on suspicion of conspiring to commit "the most serious of crimes that harm state security."

Israeli authorities say cult members planned to provoke police into a bloody shootout that cult members believed would trigger the second coming of Christ.

Concerned Christian leader Monte Kim Miller, who vanished last fall and whose whereabouts are unknown, has given his followers Biblical references that he says predict his death on the streets of Jerusalem in December 1999.

The Israeli Ministry of the Interior ordered the deportation of the 11 other cult members. However, the U.S. State Department said it could confirm just nine deportation orders for the women and children.

The three men are John Bayles of Denver, Eric Malesic, 36, of Westminster and Terry Smith, 42, of Eagle. At separate hearings, they were ordered held for 48 hours while police complete their investigation. Bayles was placed under suicide watch, police said. The first to appear in court Monday, Bayles was denied a public defender but Malesic and Smith both received counsel.

"I'm not here to hurt anybody. I don't feel I pose a threat to anybody," Bayles said.

The three men, along with two other males, would be deported after the investigation against them was completed, police said. U.S. officials have not yet been allowed to see the men but have visited the women and children, who are in "good condition," a state department spokeswoman said.

The three women and six children — one just a month old — were being held in a staff dormitory run by border police, the spokeswoman said. It's unknown when they would be deported or where they would be sent.

The crackdown on the Colorado cult was the first action taken against an extremist religious group by the Israeli government as the turn of the millennium approaches. Israel has established a task force to track groups that may seek their doomsday dreams in the Holy Land.

The action was criticized by an American director of a private agency in Jerusalem as overzealous.

The raid "was just an excuse to get them out of the Israeli government's hair," said David Parsons, director of the International Christian Embassy in Jerusalem.

"Their three-month visitors' visas had expired so it gave the government an excuse to deport them," he said.

Rumors are rampant in Jerusalem "that the city will be flooded with a lot of crazy Christians" during 1999, Parsons said. Early news reports about the 14 arrests quoted Israeli officials as saying the Concerned Christians might stage some suicide event near the Western Wall., holy to Jews, or the Temple Mount, holy to Muslims. The Temple Mount includes the El-Aqsa Mosque and the dome of the Rock, from which Muslims believe Mohammed ascended to heaven for one night.

A Hebrew language newspaper in Jerusalem reported in Monday's edition that security around the Temple Mount is extraordinary.

Meanwhile, friends and family of cult members watched TV, surfed the Internet and called one another hoping for news about their missing loved ones.

Anne Biondo, mother of cult member Annie Biondo Malesic, discovered that she had a grandchild after seeing a photo of her daughter in a newspaper.

"'That's my Annie.' That's the way she put it," said Mark Roggeman, a Denver police officer who tracks the cult and talked to Anne Biondo on Monday.

"There's a lot of mixed feelings," Roggeman said. "She's relieved, No. 1, because we've had no word of them and even seeing a picture of her daughter brought some relief. The other part is getting them to come back to this country, to see that they have an opportunity to leave the group."

Tom Clark, whose daughter Maleen is married to cult member Steve Malesic, once employed both Steve and Eric Malesic. Clark described Eric, one of the three men being held by Israeli authorities, as "just a very quiet, spiritual young man." But he said the Malesic brothers are strongly under the sway of Kim Miller. The recent developments have left Clark with a heightened sense of anxiety about his daughter and four grandchildren, all under age 7.

"I've watched (Miller) go on a progression from just a minister to somebody who is God," said Clark. "And I suspect he's gone further. That's generally the way these things go. When he gets more peculiar, I worry more about my grandbabies and daughter."

James Van Beek, an investigator in the Eagle County Sheriff's Department, has been researching the cult since his brother-in-law, James Dyck, disappeared. Dyck's father-in-law, Terry Smith, was one of the three men arrested and detained by Israeli authorities.

"Is Kim Miller putting a spin on this to make it look like evil working against their good?" Van Beek said. "I don't know. But it's a good thing we finally know where they're at. We'll be looking at where they're deported to, and maybe meet them. I just want to let them know that if they want to, they can come home."

Members of the Concerned Christians began selling their Colorado homes last fall and relatives reported them missing. Although some members are still in contact with their families in the United States, most are secretive and only say they will continue to follow Miller.

A native of Burlington, Miller, 44, told his followers that God speaks through him.

The cult's two expensive suburban homes in Jerusalem were empty on Monday. Police had searched the garden at one of the homes, but it was not clear what they were seeking. Neighbors had reported that there were four holes in the garden, dug by the residents, each hole about 18 inches in diameter.

Neighbors told police the residents of the homes were quiet, never left the area and food was brought to them.

-30-

7. Edit and/or trim the following wire stories according to directions from your instructor. Recommend a way to add a local dimension, if appropriate.

a. Teen survey

BY LINDSEY TANNER
THE ASSOCIATED PRESS

CHICAGO – A survey of teen drinking found good news and bad news — more than half of the youths ages 16 to 19 said they drank during the preceding month, but nearly two-thirds said they always appoint a designated driver.

Still, even the good news in Tuesday's study had a twist: 80 percent think it's fine to drink as long as there is a designated driver, and nearly half think that designated drivers can still drink.

"We're not impressing on kids the fact that getting drunk can be dangerous," said Dr. Richard Heyman, a Cincinnati pediatrician and chairman of the substance abuse committee at the American Academy of Pediatrics, which released the study. The telephone survey, conducted between Aug. 24 and Sept. 3, has a margin of error of plus or minus 4 percentage points.

The survey showed that nearly 30 percent of teens down six or more drinks each outing. Fifty-one percent said they consume between two and five drinks at a sitting. Eighty percent think it's OK to drink with friends as long as there is a designated driver.

"Teens have the unfortunate misconception that if they designate a driver, they can still drink as much as they like," said Dr. Joseph R. Zanga, the academy's president.

-30-

b. Wolves

BY V. DION HAYNES
KNIGHT RIDDER TRIBUNE

ALPINE, Ariz. – At the beginning of this century, the Mexican gray wolf was considered a nuisance and a threat to the quest of new settlers to transform barren tracts of land into what is now one of the most renowned cattle production regions of the country.

With the blessing of the federal government, ranchers virtually wiped out the species, paying bounties of up to $50 apiece.

Today, the tables have turned. A reward of $50,000 is being offered for information leading to the capture of whoever was responsible for the recent shooting deaths of four Mexican wolves, part of a controversial federal program to re-establish the species in the Southwest after a 50-year absence. A fifth wolf was shot to death by a camper who said the animal lunged at him.

The shootings have shattered the tranquility of the agricultural community in southeastern Arizona and deepened animosities between the federal government, ranchers and environmentalists.

Last week, after a brief period in which federal officials recaptured the surviving wolves from the 11 originally released, the U.S. Fish and Wildlife Service kicked off the second year of the program by transporting four addition wolves from breeding facilities into a holding pen near Apache National Forest. After spending a month or two getting acclimated to the area, the wolves will be released into the wild.

"In the face of adversity with all the shootings, I think we're in pretty good shape," said David Parsons, the Fish and Wildlife Services' Mexican wolf recovery leader. "The wolves performed better than expected. The most significant impediment to recovery is human-caused mortality."

Investigators from federal and state wildlife agencies have been unable to solve the shootings, which occurred between April and November last year, but federal officials say they are following several leads.

Ranchers, who vehemently opposed the project as a threat to their livestock, believe the government assumes one of them was responsible for the shootings.

"There is a $100,000 fine for shooting a wolf" that is protected by the Endangered Species Act, said Earl Baker, a longtime cattle rancher from nearby

Springerville. "And if you're a convicted felon, you can't hold a Forest Service grazing permit. Ranchers have too much to lose (to kill the wolves)."

Instead, they believe the wolves either were shot by hunters who mistook the animals for coyotes, or by environmentalists who wanted to put pressure on the ranchers and draw more attention to the program.

Animosities between environmentalists and ranchers surfaced last week when several members of the group Defenders of Wildlife crashed the American Farm Bureau Federation's annual convention in Albuquerque. Group members, accompanied by a Mexican wolf on a leash, protested the Farm Bureau's opposition to a similar wolf restoration project at Yellowstone National Park.

"At its heart, the controversy (by the ranchers) has little to do with the wolf and mostly involves baggage put on the wolf," said Craig Miller, southwest representative for Defenders of Wildlife, which posted the reward.

The group also has offered to compensate ranchers who lose livestock to wolves. So far, wolves have attacked a horse and killed a guard dog, but no livestock.

"It's all about the ranchers' mistrust of the government, private property rights and control issues," Miller said.

The Mexican wolf population had dwindled to about seven by the 1970s. By 1978, federal officials had captured all the surviving wolves, which by then had been listed as endangered, and launched a long-term project to re-establish the population.

Over the years, the number of facilities around the country that breed the Mexican wolf grew from one to about 40, and the number of wolves grew to nearly 200. Federal Fish and Wildlife Service officials waited until the ranks of wolves reached that level before releasing the first group into the wild early last year. The goal of the project is to have 100 wolves living in the wilds of Arizona and New Mexico by 2005.

Three weeks after the first group of 11 wolves were released last March, "two pups knocked down an elk," said Parsons of the Fish and Wildlife Service. "Eventually, all the wolves were ... hunting. We thought we would have had to continue feeding them."

He added that officials at the agency were also pleased by the fact that two female wolves had gotten pregnant, something they hadn't expected so soon given that the animals were still getting accustomed to their new environment.

-30-

c. Timber

BY DAVE MORANTZ
THE ASSOCIATED PRESS

TRENTON, S.C. – Steve Cantrell's minivan idles along row after row of raised topsoil beds containing millions of tree seedlings, each poking about a foot high to make the beds stretch like strips of plus green carpet to the horizon.

As he drives along, however, the supervisor of the state-run Taylor Forest Tree Nursery near Trenton notes where the beds are marred by splotches of brown dirt.

Last winter it was floods. This summer and fall it was drought. The result is dead pine seedlings, just as a strong economy and soaring timber prices have landowners demanding more young trees to plant.

Cantrell says he gets calls daily from landowners wanting seedlings. Spindly loblolly pine seedlings cost $36 per thousand; hardy white and longleaf pine seedlings cost twice that much. Most years he can fill orders, even from those who wait until the last minute.

This time, he said, "landowners may have to wait, unfortunately, until next year."

They are landowners like J.M. Pendarvis, who spent more than $50,000 to prepare about 220 acres near Edgefield for planting this year.

"I'm not holding out too much hope," he says. "If we don't get the seedlings, we'll lose all these acres."

Pendarvis owns about 2,500 acres around Edgefield and Estill. After calling state nurseries and timber companies across the Southeast for more than a month, he finally found seedlings this week. He had to travel to Statesboro, Ga., to pick them up.

Clearing each acre costs about $200. Pendarvis says that if he did not find the seedlings, he would have lost about $55 an acre, $12,000 overall, by fertilizing land that would have gone unused.

The U.S. Agricultural Department says about 5,000 acres of nonindustrial private forest land in South Carolina need replanting at a cost of about $625,000. Those who own such land can sell the timber but cannot make forest-related products, like furniture or paper.

It takes a loblolly pine about 35 years to mature fully, while white and longleaf pines take a few years longer.

The seedling supply has been tight for the past few years as a strong economy has increased demand for timber, said Guy SanFrantello, who retired in December as head of the Forestry Commission division that includes its tree nurseries.

The cost of 1,000 board feet of timber, an industry standard, averaged $291 this past year, down from $337 the year before but still up from $274 five years ago.

-30-

CHAPTER 8

Making a long story short: Editing for brevity and clarity

With editorial space and readers' time at a premium, shorter stories have become increasingly popular. But it's important not to sacrifice clarity or fairness for brevity. For example, if you trim that explanatory paragraph, will the reader understand a technical term used in the story? Are you merely trimming a repetitive passage or deleting a transition? Have you cut out the quotes that add fairness and balance to a story about a controversial issue or a political race? These are just a few of the pitfalls in trimming stories.

As a copy editor, you should be on the lookout for ways to tighten copy without harming it. Sometimes you eliminate or reduce background material, for example. Or you might delete a quotation that essentially echoes paraphrasing (or vice versa).

On a feature, or a story involving a particularly sensitive issue, it might be wise to confer with the assigning editor or the reporter before whacking away. Some newsrooms have a policy allowing no more than a 10 percent trim by a copy editor without such consultation. Certain information that may seem extraneous to the copy editor might be considered crucial to the reporter who is privy to more details and background.

Besides trimming stories to fit the available space, copy editors often are assigned to take several stories, usually from wire services, and rewrite them into a roundup of short items. Roundups, or briefs columns, offer snapshots of the news, or perhaps the print version of "sound bites." They represent a space-saving way of getting a wider sampling of stories into the daily news. Some newspapers also do a weekly briefs column that summarizes highlights of the week's top stories.

Some stories lend themselves to this treatment better than others. Breaking, "hard" news with who-what-when summary leads are the best candidates. Feature stories, with anecdotal or scene-setting leads are not as appropriate. News judgment also comes into play: Some stories are obviously worth more space and a larger headline than a brief allows. Space for news varies day to day, depending on advertising. So a story that might be run in its entirety on a day with more room may be reduced to three paragraphs if the paper is "tight."

Even if you are working to turn a 12-inch hard-news, inverted-pyramid wire story into a three-paragraph national news brief, you can't necessarily just lop off all but the first three paragraphs and stick a headline on it. You have to make sure the copy is as complete as possible, that it includes the most important details from the story, and that it reads smoothly. You also need to make sure the location is identified within the brief, unless your publication includes datelines with each brief. And, if the brief is based on a continuing story, you may need to give a sentence or two of background information to put the latest development into context.

Since each brief may not have a dateline or byline, it's also important that you remember to give the proper credit, such as "Associated Press" or "From Wire Reports" at the top or bottom of the briefs roundup. In the case of local briefs, credit "From Staff Reports."

The following exercises will give you practice in shortening stories and selecting and editing news briefs.

Exercises

1. Look through five consecutive issues of one newspaper and choose three developing, continuing news stories. For each of these stories, write a three-paragraph news summary, emphasizing the latest developments in the story, but including enough background detail so a reader who missed the earlier stories would be brought up-to-date.

2. Find five full stories in a newspaper that would be appropriate for a national roundup, and edit each into a two- or three-paragraph news brief.

3. Look through the local newspaper, and list five examples you find of wordiness and/or redundancy and your suggestions for rewording. Then choose one story to shorten by eliminating wordiness or by deleting extraneous details or quotations. Count the number of words you could save in the story. Does the audience make a difference in what you could omit? Explain.

4. Trim the following stories according to the specific directions for each story.

   a. Denver riot: Trim this 840-word story to 750 words, or a length specified by your instructor. Make a note of details that could be omitted if the article were appearing in a publication in or near the Denver area.

   BY JULIE CART AND J. R. MOEHRINGER
   TIMES STAFF WRITERS

   DENVER—This city howled under a full moon Sunday, reveling as its beloved Broncos repeated as world champions, defeating the Atlanta Falcons, 34-19, in Super Bowl XXXIII at Miami.

   There was also a repeat of the raucous celebrations that trashed the downtown area after last year's win. Even though authorities here had warned for a week that police would immediately move to quash unruliness, fans poured into the LoDo area of Denver's revitalized downtown and broke storefront windows and set fires.

   After the game, several hundred rowdy fans spilled out of restaurants and bars and converged on historic Larimer Square, overrunning police lines. Police pulled back and contained the mob on one block, and watched as fans turned a fashionable shopping street into a mosh pit.

Fans climbed light poles, rode on each other's shoulders and grabbed the early editions of local papers being sold on street corners. They used them to build bonfires.

Police watched for about 30 minutes before moving in with riot gear. Forming two lines, they advanced on the crowd, striding forward, shoulder to shoulder. Wearing gas masks and helmets and carrying riot shields, police fired canisters of tear gas, forcing the crowd into retreat through the acrid cloud.

Crowds also gathered at the state Capitol and were rebuffed several times by police using tear gas.

But even with the scattered disturbances, police did not characterize the celebrations as riots, and no arrests were reported.

Last year, about 30,000 revelers poured into the downtown area, and, before the night was through, stores were vandalized, cars were burned and 60 people were injured.

Given the passion the Broncos engender here, such exuberance was to be expected. During the week, "Locally Owned" signs sprouted in store windows—merchants' code for "Please don't break our windows."

But not all celebrations got out of hand. Michelle Cornel and Chris Matos drove from Boulder to watch the game at a downtown bar. The two were hurrying after the game to skirt the crowds, even as they joined in the cheering cries of "Go Broncos!"

"It was awesome, totally awesome," said Cornel, who wore an orange-and-blue "Cat in the Hat" style Broncos hat. "Of course, I never doubted we wouldn't win. But it sure felt good. Two-peat!"

Matos was distracted by revelers wearing plastic horse heads, standard Bronco regalia. "Man, it was almost a boring game," he said. "But, weeeeee wooonnn!"

Even as Super Bowl parties were in full roar in usually quiet neighborhoods, many businesses closed early Sunday, or never opened.

Larimer Square, epicenter of last year's riot, girded itself this time. Trash cans and benches were lashed to light poles. The restaurants that remained open served beverages in plastic cups. And suspended guide wires strung across the street were taken down. Last year, the thick wire served as a trapeze for rambunctious fans.

The Broncos will be feted today during a parade and rally. To accommodate the team's youngest fans, Denver public schools will allow children attending the festivities to miss school and count it as an excused absence.

Super Bowl Sunday in Atlanta started bad and got worse.

First, Falcon fans woke to the news that one of their star players, Eugene Robinson, was arrested the night before on a sex solicitation charge. Then the weather turned ugly, with icy rain that cast a pall on Super Bowl parties.

Finally, cable TV went out all over Atlanta, so countless fans couldn't even watch the debacle.

Police closed off streets in the ritzy Buckhead section, expecting either wild celebrations or raucous grieving, particularly when fans began lining up early in the morning outside sports bars and restaurants. But the dreary weather and the Falcons' performance made for a quiet, early night.

"I'm going to go home and cry in my pillow," said Tami Howard, a data processor, standing under an umbrella on Peachtree Road just minutes after the last dispiriting play. "I'm very proud of them, but I can't help but be depressed."

Penn Wells, a banker and native Atlantan, flew in from his home in Dallas to watch the game. He wanted to be in Atlanta for the inevitable victory parties. After sitting for eight hours at John Harvard's Brew House, wearing his Dirty Bird T-shirt, even watching through all the pre-game shows, he was in a post-game gloom.

"   We're encouraged," he said, not sounding at all encouraged. "After 33 years of fruitless play, we're in the Super Bowl. So, maybe next year. ... You never know."

Sally Tabb, a peanut farmer from southern Georgia, also sounded a hopeful note. "This was just a warmup for 2000," she said, referring to next year's Super Bowl in Atlanta, "when we'll be the home team."

-30-

b. Avalanches: Trim this 625-word story to 500 words, or according to your instructor's directions.

BY RANDOLPH E. SCHMID
THE ASSOCIATED PRESS

WASHINGTON — "Detached snow drags the men into the abyss and snow falling rapidly from high summits engulfs the living squadrons," wrote the poet Silius Italicus in one of the earliest reports of deadly Alpine avalanches.

He wrote of snowslides that devastated Hannibal's invading army in 218 B.C., but fatal avalanches in recent weeks prove the danger remains for those living in and passing through the Alps.

Europe is enduring its snowiest winter in a half-century as fresh snow piles atop crusts of old snow, the formula for deadly avalanches. Austria and Switzerland have been especially hard hit.

The toll, though, is unlikely ever to top the losses of the Italian and Austrian troops who fought four years of bitter battles in the Tyrol region during World War I.

From 1914 to 1918, avalanche deaths in both armies may have topped 40,000, according to the book "Darkest Hours," by Jay Robert Nash. In one incident alone, Dec. 12, 1916, snow swept away an Austrian barracks, killing 253.

"The mountains in winter are more dangerous than the Italians," Austrian Matthias Zdarsky wrote of the battles.

Two thousand years earlier, the African general Hannibal Barca might have had the same thought. Roman historians record that Hannibal lost 18,000 men,

2,000 horses and several elephants crossing the mountains to invade Italy from the north.

It isn't just the military that suffers, of course.

On Jan. 20, 1951, for example, an estimated 240 people died when accumulated snows gave way following a series of heavy rains, sweeping down on a dozen towns in Austria, Italy and Switzerland. Nineteen died in Vals, Switzerland the hardest hit village and six snowslides within an hour devastated the Swiss town of Andermatt, killing 13.

'"The only signal the avalanches gave was the sound of hurricanelike winds that preceded the rush of millions of tons of snow, which quickly snapped off the thousands of trees that had been planted to prevent just such an occurrence," Nash reports.

Hundreds of years earlier, at midnight on Saturday, Jan. 16, 1602, "a hideously gruesome avalanche smashed into the town of Davos," wrote Swiss chronicler Flury Sprecher von Bernegg, quoted in "The Avalanche Book" by Betsy Armstrong and Knox Williams.

"The rescuers were summoned by the ringing of church bells. The rescue effort continued for three days and three nights. ...Thirteen people were found dead under the snow; seven in one house, four in a church. A 14-year-old girl was found alive after being buried in the snow for 36 hours," von Bernegg wrote.

Twenty-seven people died in 1869 when an avalanche struck Biel, Switzerland. One family a husband and wife and four children — were hurled bodily into the street, still in their beds, historians say.

And there were 84 fatalities among the 200 residents of Obergesteln, Switzerland, when an avalanche struck on Feb. 20, 1720, Robert Henson reports in the January-February edition of the magazine Weatherwise.

On Jan. 17, 1718, a wall of snow destroyed every house in the Swiss village of Leukerbad, killing 52 people. Two centuries earlier, in 1518, 61 died when snow engulfed the same hamlet.

Other major Alpine avalanches with 100 or more fatalities include:

- 1499, avalanche killed 400 in mercenary army in Great St. Bernard Pass, Switzerland. They were en route to attack Milan.
- 1598, Graubunden, Switzerland, avalanche, 100 deaths.
- 1606, Davos-Frauenkirch, Switzerland, 100 killed.
- 1689, Montafon Valley, Austria, 300 killed.
- 1755, 200 killed in avalanches in German, French and Italian Alps.
- 1799, hundreds of Russian soldiers killed in snowslide at Panixer Pass, Switzerland.
- 1954, avalanches in the German, Italian and Austrian Alps killed a total of 145.

-30-

c. Ventura: Trim this 740-word book review to 500 words, or a length specified by your instructor.

By Kurt Jensen
Me: By Jimmy (Big Boy) Valente
By Garrison Keillor
Viking, 152 pp., $ 15.95

Jesse Ventura had not been elected Minnesota governor more than a week before Garrison Keillor was wryly comparing him to the likes of Louisiana's Earl Long and Georgia's Lester Maddox in the pages of Time. Clearly, the state's satirist laureate has found inspiration in Ventura's long-haul truculence and has even made his presence a regular on A Prairie Home Companion.

In *Me: By Jimmy (Big Boy) Valente*, Keillor writes with the ease of a man freed from torpor, channeling his storytelling skills and keen eye for absurdity into a fictional "as told to" autobiography of a professional wrestler who just happens to be the new governor of Minnesota.

But the blunt Ventura hasn't spawned another *All the King's Men*. Keillor's novella, seeking laughs, instead experiments with a taut comic-book style. Think Sergeant Rock, the DC Comics classic.

Me also is cut from the same cloth as Keillor's *The Book of Guys*, with its familiar theme of adventurers who have longed to find fame and fortune (mostly fame) away from their stifling hometowns and have deeply reflective lives. It is doubtful that Ventura has ever described himself, as Valente does, as "the first modern existential wrestler."

Keillor might well be describing his own success when Valente calls his election "a breakthrough for a boy from Minnesota, a state of Lutherans, a people who don't believe in flaunting the goods or fighting to win. They believe in being humble and learning to accept it. It is not a showbiz state. ... It is a state of folks in earth tones. I broke the mold."

Valente's saga unfolds briskly. Born illegitimate, adopted and named Clifford Oxnard in Minneapolis, he joins the Navy's elite WALRUS (Water Air Land Rising Up Suddenly) team and is off to Vietnam, where, on his very first day, he captures a Viet Cong soldier who is to become his lifelong professional enemy, known as The Rodent.

After leaving the service, Valente moves to Alaska and lucks into professional wrestling. And when the promoter announces "the show needs a fairy," his future is assured. The massive but nimble Valente evolves from the boa-wearing Flower Child to the managing partner of his wrestling circuit and takes pride in introducing sweat-seeking cruise missiles and giant trucks to the shows.

Keillor has neatly distilled the appeal of professional wrestling, with its outrageous rhetoric and stereotypes, to its fans. Knowing they are fungible in the modern workplace, "what they miss more than anything is pure chauvinism, which is anathema in the economy because it hinders productivity, but people miss it, that old atavism, the blood lust, and living in a society of anonymity among the Burger Kings and Barnes and Nobles, they need hatred to give them a sense of belonging, and that's where we come in. We're metaphors and icons, a beacon in their dim lives, creators of moral fables!"

So, naturally, Valente's winning ways let him energize a lackluster governor's race, although his recruitment by the Ethical Party and subsequent campaign are dispatched fairly quickly in the last few pages.

Flush with victory, Valente eyes taking on Al Gore in the 2000 presidential race, which lets Keillor launch his sharpest political riff.

"You're obsolete, Al," Valente crows. "The fringe is the center now. TV has made a joke of politics and a joker like me can beat a stuffed owl like you. You are living in the nineteenth century when the president stood at a lectern and read a speech in a big pipe-organ voice and everyone listened and nobody's dog barked. Those days are gone."

Me is more virtuoso wordplay than trenchant satire, but, distressingly, it contains Keillor's first, and let's hope last, racist caricature in The Rodent, who speaks in a stereotyped Asian dialect not seen much since the end of World War II. Although Keillor's ghostwriter occasionally steps outside Valente's narration to make some jokes at his subject's expense — there's a splendid running gag on the use of "pellucid," for instance — he allows Valente to spew The Rodent's slurred consonants without a trace of disapproval or detachment. That's lazy for a writer of Keillor's skill, and Valente's offhand apology at the end doesn't erase the taint.

-30-

5. Compile the following stories into a roundup of local news briefs, each no longer than three paragraphs:

   a. Vest

   Police say a bullet-proof vest likely saved the life of a Spring Valley officer, who was recovering today after the vest deflected a gunman's bullet away from his heart.

   Declaring him a "real hero," police said Lt. Connor O'Riley interrupted the suspect and two possible accomplices as they beat and tried to rape a 25-year-old woman. The assailants remained at-large.

   The woman, her body battered and face pistol-whipped, is lucky to be alive, police said. "These people are extremely dangerous," said Lt. Michael Murphy, department spokesman. "When you have a suspect willing to kill a uniformed police officer, they have to be considered dangerous."

   The shooting left the department shaken, as O'Riley became just the second officer in over a decade to be wounded in the line of duty. Sgt. Jesus Gonzalez was shot in the forearm during the execution of a search warrant 12 years earlier.

   "All of our officers put their lives on the line on a daily basis," Murphy said. "And over the years, we've had lots of officers get shot at, but through training and the grace of God, we have not become victims. When something like this happens, it makes us remember we're all vulnerable."

   The incident began at 11:45 p.m. Monday when officers were dispatched to the Park Hill Apartments on North Park Hill Road on an assault-in-progress call. A woman was attacked in an area just north of the apartment complex and dragged inside the building where the assailants continued beating her, police records show.

   As Murphy, a 15-year veteran, entered the building, a man walked out and fired two shots from a handgun, striking Murphy in the left hand and left side of his chest. A big bruise formed beneath Murphy's vest where the bullet hit, O'Riley said. "He definitely could have died if the bullet would have penetrated," he said. Murphy returned fire as the suspect fled but it wasn't known if the bullets hit or missed their target. Murphy and the woman were taken to Memorial Hospital, where both were listed in good condition and were expected to be released late today.

-30-

b. Blood

The Red Cross will hold an emergency blood drive at it's chapter headquarters Friday from 9-5 to restock dangerously low supplies.

Recent disasters and dips in donations have resulted in dangerously low supplies in the region, according to Adelle Brown, a spokeswoman for the local chapter. Inclement weather is blamed primarily for the drop in donations, she added.

Blood supplies around the nation have been strained recently by natural disasters, including tornadoes and flooding in the Midwest that have claimed many lives and injured scores of victims, Brown noted.

"When one of these natural disasters strikes, we're called on to pull together and meet that urgent need, but it takes a toll on our supplies," she said. "Now we need to restock because we would really be in dire straights if another disaster should hit anytime soon."

Brown said that Red Cross volunteers will be standing by Friday to provide transportation for donors who need it. Those who wish to make an appointment may call 555-HELP, Brown said.

Also, The Old-Fashioned Churn is donating coupons for free ice cream to those donating blood for the first time.

The Friday blood drive is in addition to the regular weekly collection, which takes place at the chapter headquarters, Brown said. "We're hoping for a really big turnout to boost our supplies," she said.

-30-

c. Fire

Fire totally destroyed an abandoned barn in Northwoods Township last night and burned about an acre of brush before it was extinguished by Northwoods volunteer firefighters.

About 20 firefighters responded to the blaze, which was reported by a neighbor who saw smoke and flames coming from the area at about 7 p.m. and called 911. It took about an hour to put out the fire.

No one was injured, and a nearby farmhouse was not damaged.

The cause of the fire is under investigation, but fire Capt. Howie Moshowitz said it is believed that a cigarette thrown by a passing motorist may have ignited the blaze.

There was no immediate estimate of the damage. The barn's owner, Cecilia Davis, who lives in the nearby farmhouse but was not home at the time of the fire, said the barn had been empty for years. "I feel very lucky," she said. "I don't think there was a thing in it except maybe some old magazines and a broken lawn mower."

-30-

d. Hit-run

Police are seeking information about a hit-and-run accident that occurred Monday at the Quik Stop on Buehler Lane.

At about 5 p.m., according to police, a small red car struck the left side of a white Chevrolet sport-utility vehicle just as that vehicle's driver was pulling into the convenience store's parking lot, and then quickly drove off.

Police said the owner of the Chevrolet was unable to get a good luck at the car's license plate or the driver, which he thinks was a young man. The car's rear fender was dented and the left tail light smashed, according to the police report.

Anyone who might have witnessed the accident or have any information is asked to call the police at 555-1000. There is a reward for information leading to an arrest.

-30-

e. Recycling

Mayor Sydney Delacroix has appointed a new director of recycling for the city.

George Campanella, 38, formerly manager of transportation for the city's Sanitation Department, was named to replace Marcia Thomas, who plans to retire at the end of the month after 10 years in the position.

Campanella says he hopes to raise citizens' awareness of recycling efforts and improve the efficiency of collection. "I expect my background in managing the fleet of garbage trucks, as well as my knowledge of the city, to come in handy," he said during a press conference at which his promotion was announced.

Participation in recycling is down, Campanella noted. Five years ago, Spring Valley residents were recycling about 10 percent of their residential trash, including glass, paper, alumnium, steel and plastics. That has declined to only about 8 percent.

Campanella says he wants to study the situation in depth before making any changes, but he is considering expanding the area served by weekly curbside pickup, and plastics might be dropped from the program to save money.

Currently, some neighborhoods, particularly in the eastern areas, have no curbside pickup, residents must drop off recyclables at collection centers, which are often vandalized, Campanella noted.

-30-

6. Compile the following stories into a roundup of national news briefs, each no longer than three paragraphs:

a. Explosion

DEARBORN, Mich. (AP) — An explosion and fire at a power station for a huge Ford Motor Co. plant killed one worker and injured several others yesterday as crews battled the blaze for hours.

Three workers were unaccounted for, the company said.

"This is the worst day of my life," chairman William Clay Ford said.

Fire broke out about 1 p.m. at the coal-fired plant at Ford's huge River Route complex.

The plant produces electricity for the entire complex, generating enough power to serve a city the size of Boston, Ford spokesman Michael Vaughn said.

The cause of the fire was being investigated.

Oakwood Hospital treated 11 patients from the fire and transferred 10 others elsewhere because of the severity of their burns, said Dr. Gary Christopher, director of emergency services at Oakwood.

Garden City Hospital received one patient, public relations director Terry Carroll said. Carol Craig, a spokeswoman for the University of Michigan Hospital, said the hospital was expecting five patients, some from Oakwood, at its burn unit.

A spokeswoman for Michigan Consolidated Gas Co. said that gas was shut off at the complex, a standard procedure, and that there was no evidence the explosion was gas-related.

About 4,000 employees were present at the time, Ford spokesman Jim Vella said.

The 1,100-acre Rouge complex was once the world's largest auto plant. Henry Ford built it in 1918, dreaming of assembling a car from start to finish in one location.

At its peak in the 1940s, 85,000 people worked at the plant in Dearborn, about seven miles west of Detroit. About 10,000 people work at the six Ford factories still in operation at the Rouge, where Ford builds Mustangs.

-30-

b. Auction

BY MICHAEL MILLER
REUTERS

LOS ANGELES — An auction to sell O.J. Simpson's Heisman Trophy and other sports memorabilia seized from him to satisfy a wrongful-death judgment will take place on the Internet as well as conventionally.

The event, being conducted by Butterfield & Butterfield in Los Angeles, will be one of the first major auctions to take online bids.

Michael Schwartz, Butterfield & Butterfield's director of entertainment memorabilia, said yesterday that he expected "tens of thousands, if not more" Internet bidders to join in.

The Feb. 16 event will also operate on a more traditional level, with bidders on the floor and others making offers by telephone.

Simpson's property will be auctioned as part of a court-ordered sale to meet a $32.5 million civil judgment against him in the 1994 stabbing deaths of his ex-wife, Nicole Brown Simpson and her friend Ronald Goldman.

Simpson was acquitted of murder charges but was later found civilly liable for their deaths.

Butterfield & Butterfield is holding the auction in conjunction with Yahoo Inc. and Livebid.com. Schwartz said Yahoo would be the server, while the technology that makes the live online bidding possible would be provided by Livebid.com.

According to the catalog, the auction house expects most items to fetch in the hundreds of dollars.

Simpson's Heisman Trophy, which he won in 1968 as the nation's best college football player while playing for the University of Southern California, is the jewel in the crown and is expected to fetch at least $100,000.

The other fairly high-priced item is the official certificate presented to Simpson in 1985 when he was inducted into the Football Hall of Fame. It is expected to sell for between $5,000 and $10,000.

Other personal property seized from Simpson's former Brentwood mansion and going on sale includes furniture, rugs, paintings and several Tiffany-style lamps.

Schwartz said online bidders could preregister by going to the auction house's Web page, http://www.butterfields.com

-30-

c. Strokes

BY DANIEL Q. HANEY
THE ASSOCIATED PRESS

NASHVILLE — For the first time, doctors have shown that they can reverse massive strokes up to six hours after the start of symptoms by squirting a new clot-dissolving medicine directly into the brain.

The approach offers potentially better treatment for the worst strokes and a doubling of the three-hour window that is now the deadline for people to get help before they suffer permanent brain damage.

Doctors tested the medicine, called prourokinase, on people who suffered a particularly serious form of stroke that accounts for about one-third of the 600,000 strokes treated in this country annually.

"If you have a massive stroke, this gives you the best chance of a decent outcome," said Seven R. Levine, a Detroit Medical Center doctor who was not involved in the study.

Until two years ago, strokes were totally untreatable in the hours immediately after they occurred. Then researchers discovered that TPA, or tissue plasminogen activator, already the mainstay of treating heart attacks, could also dissolve the blood clots that cause most strokes.

But researchers suggested that TPA could help only if given within three hours of the start of symptoms, and brain scans are necessary to make sure the stroke truly results from a clot. Even then, there is about a 6 percent chance that TPA will trigger bleeding that makes the stroke worse.

Largely because of these difficulties, TPA is given to only about 5 percent of stroke victims.

The results of the prourokinase study, directed by Dr. Anthony J. Furlan of the Cleveland Clinic Foundation, were released yesterday at a stroke conference sponsored by the American Heart Association. The study was financed by Abbott Laboratories, which is developing the drug.

Prourokinase may be more effective if it is released via a catheter, threaded through an artery, directly into the brain. TPA is injected into a vein and must travel throughout the body.

At 51 hospitals in the United States and Canada, 180 patients who suffered blockages of the brain's middle cerebral artery were given either prourokinase or a blood thinner called heparin, which was not expected to have a significant effect. Symptoms started between three and six hours earlier.

Researchers found that, three months later, 40 percent of the patients getting prourokinase had little or no disability resulting from their strokes, compared with 25 percent receiving heparin. Twenty-four percent of the prourokinase patients died, as did 27 percent in the comparison group.

"This will be the second major revolution in stroke treatment in this decade," predicted Dr. Randall Higashida of the University of California, San Francisco, who took part in the study.

He said it could be widely used at most major medical centers. Furlan said he hoped the federal officials would approve prourokinase for routine use by early next year. He could not estimate its cost.

-30-

d. Executions

BY ROCHELLE HINES

THE ASSOCIATED PRESS

McALESTER, Okla. — A man who killed his mother, his stepfather and a store clerk when he was 16 was put to death early yesterday after telling his family that his execution would do nothing to change their feelings.

"All the people who are hating me right now and are here waiting to see me die, when you wake up in the morning, you aren't going to feel any different," Sean Sellers said before he was executed by injection at the Oklahoma State Penitentiary.

"Reach out to God and He will hear you," Sellers said. "Let Him touch your hearts. Don't hate all your lives."

It marked the first time in 40 years an American was put to death for crimes committed at age 16.

A short time earlier, a hitchhiker who beat, robbed and killed a man by running him over with his own car and stabbing him more than 30 times with a screwdriver was executed by injection in Arizona.

Darick Gerlaugh, 38, was the seventh American Indian executed in the United States since the death penalty was restored in 1976 and the first permitted to use a sweat lodge for purification ceremonies.

Gerlaugh had no last words.

Sellers' final words angered relatives who witnessed his execution.

"He took his last dig at us. ... It is very presumptuous that he would know how we would still feel," stepsister Noelle Terry said.

Sellers, 29, killed a convenience store clerk shortly after his 16th birthday and, six months later, his mother and stepfather, Wand and Paul Bellofatto.

"Sean's been not a part of our family since he decided to pull the trigger on our father and his mother," stepbrother Lorne Bellofatto said. "Pretty much he's been dead to us since then."

Gerlaugh was one of three men convicted of kidnapping, robbing and killing Scott Schwartz, 22, in 1980. The three were hitchhiking from Chandler to Phoenix and planned to rob whoever stopped to pick them up.

While the two other men held Schwartz down, Gerlaugh repeatedly ran over him with his car, then helped stab him.

-30-

e. Quotas

BY TOM KIRCHOFER
THE ASSOCIATED PRESS

BOSTON — After considering the fragility of school affirmative-action programs nationwide, the Boston School Committee will not challenge a court ruling that overturned a race-based admissions policy for one of its most prestigious schools.

The committee decided Wednesday not to appeal the rejection of admission policies at the Boston Latin School by an appeals court. Officials felt the case was unlikely to win at the Supreme Court.

At a time when racial preferences are under fire, the decision points to the importance of choosing which battles are worth fighting, since an unfavorable Supreme Court decision could have undone such programs around the country, experts said.

"One of the things that the court has been most set against is quotas or anything that looks like a quote," said Richard Fallon, a constitutional scholar at Harvard Law School. "They have consistently, in all of their cases, said how skeptical they are of quotas."

The admissions system struck down last year by the appeals court admitted half of Boston Latin's students based on entrance-exam scores and grades only, while the other half were admitted based on scores, grades and race. A previously rejected plan had set aside 35 percent of seats for blacks and Hispanics.

Fallon and several other legal experts said several members of the Supreme Court, most notably Chief Justice William H. Rehnquist and Justices Antonin Scalia and Clarence Thomas, are generally seen as strongly opposed to quotas.

In the 1978 case of Bakke V. University of California, the Supreme Court struck down the use of racial quotas in school admissions but allowed schools to consider race in deciding which students to accept.

And in the last decade, the court has twice rejected set-aside plans for minority government contractors.

The Boston case centered on a ninth grader who contended in 1997 that she was denied entrance to the school despite scoring better than minorities who were admitted.

Kent Greenfield, who teaches a seminar on the Supreme Court at Boston College Law School, described the court as being in a state of flux on affirmative action.

"My guess is the reluctance to ask the court to make these decisions is a reluctance that is shared among the justices themselves," he said.

But, he said, many court observers expect that two or three justices could retire in the coming years, possibly giving the next president the ability to dramatically reshape the court's stance on affirmative action.

-30-

7. Compile the following stories into a roundup of world news briefs, each no longer than three paragraphs:

a. Arafat

WASHINGTON (AP) — Palestinian leader Yasser Arafat affirmed Wednesday he intends to carry out the stalled West Bank accords with Israel. Protests grew, meanwhile, over his planned meeting with President Clinton at a prayer breakfast.

Arafat, on a brief U.S. visit, is due to discuss peace prospects with Clinton at a prayer breakfast today. But the spokesman for the breakfast chairman, Rep. Steve Largent, R-Okla., said Largent had asked Clinton last Friday "not to politicize the breakfast by having the meeting."

The spokesman, Brad Keena, said Largent supported Arafat's attendance but disapproved of Clinton's taking up controversial issues at the breakfast with the Palestinian leader.

Hundreds of Christian leaders plan to attend the 47th breakfast sponsored by members of Congress.

But several Christian and Jewish groups have called for a boycott and accused Arafat of an unrepentant terrorist past.

"I am insistent on following up the peace process," Arafat said.

The process is stalled, with Israel refusing to yield more land until Arafat's Palestinian Authority imposes tougher restraints on terrorism and prosecutes suspects.

On another touchy subject, he said Palestinian leaders were grappling with the question of a Palestinian state. "This can't be mentioned now," Arafat said.

-30-

b. Gondola

CAVALESE, Italy (AP) — The families of the 20 people killed when a U.S. Marine jet sliced a ski gondola line demanded Tuesday that the United States compensate them for their losses.

Some 25 relatives, gathering in Italy one year after the tragedy, complained that the United States allocated $20 million to the ski resort town, while failing to give enough compensation to them.

"How could twisted metal be more important to the U.S. government than twisted bodies and lost lives?" said a statement read in four languages by members of the victims' families.

"It is clear that the United States is responsible for this accident, and it is only fair for these families to be compensated for the wrongful death of their loved ones," it said.

A EA-6B Prowler jet on a low-level training mission severed the cable of the Mount Cermis gondola line on Feb. 3, 1998.

The 20 killed were a Polish mother and son, seven German sports buddies, five Belgian classmates, two retired Italian shopkeepers, an Austrian concert violinist and railway worker, a Dutch student and the Italian cable car operator.

Defense and prosecution lawyers have agreed that the Mount Cermis ski life was not marked on the map given to the pilot, Capt. Richard Ashby, 31, of Mission Viejo, Calif.

However, prosecutors claim he was flying his aircraft too fast and too low when the jet struck and severed the cable.

-30-

c. Swiss

BY ELIZABETH OLSON
THE NEW YORK TIMES

GENEVA — The Swiss are voting today on whether to legalize everything from marijuana to heroin and cocaine, a measure that — if passed — would give Switzerland the most sweeping decriminalization of drug use, possession and production in Europe.

Government officials are warning that a yes vote could turn this tranquil A;lpine nation into a "paradise for the Mafia" and a magnet for "drug terrorists."

Proponents of the drug legalization initiative, led by a group of Socialists and medical doctors, argue that it could break up Switzerland's flourishing black market in drugs and save the country hundreds of millions of dollars in law enforcement.

They propose to give every Swiss resident over 18 an electronic credit card to withdraw a specified amount of drugs. The dosage would be set in consultation with a doctor or other medical professional, but no psychological or medical treatment would be mandated. Only those younger than 18 would be required to see a drug counselor before receiving an access card.

The card, explained a Zurich physician, David Winizki, an originator of the concept, "would be like making a withdrawal from a bank cash terminal."

"The dose would be programmed in," he continued. "The consumer would run the card with its magnetic strip through the machine and the drugstore would supply, for example, a gram of heroin for 12 Swiss francs." A gram of heroin or cocaine now costs about $36 on the street and 12 Swiss francs equals about $8.70.

Under the plan, a user could withdraw drugs daily, or up to one week's supply, for an amount lower than current street rates.

Opinion polls indicate that only about 40 percent of Swiss support the liberalization idea. That would suggest passage is unlikely. But the drug issue pervades

Switzerland, where federal statistics count between 30,000 and 36,000 narcotics addicts, most of them using heroin.

-30-

d. Africa

LISBON (AP) — Thousands of people fled the capital of Guinea-Bissau yesterday as fighting intensified between loyalist forces and rebels who threatened a "final assault" on the city. At least 15 people were reported killed.

The fighting, which restarted over the weekend in the West African country, appeared to mark the disintegration of a November peace accord that halted a five-month civil war in the former Portuguese colony.

Wagdi Othman, spokesman for the U.N. World Food Program, said most of the 300,000 residents of the capital, Bissau, were fleeing the city toward the port and interior.

At least 15 people were killed in the new fighting, the Portuguese news agency Lusa reported. It said three shells hit the main hospital in Bissau, where about 150 wounded people had been taken.

"It's carnage, a catastrophic situation," Dr. Placido Cardoso told Lusa.

Seven people were killed and 30 wounded in a Roman Catholic mission outside Bissau where hundreds of people had taken refuge, Lusa said. It was not clear if artillery fire hit the mission.

Aid workers in Bissau reported that among the wounded were members of the regional defense force ECOMOG, the defense arm of the 16-member Economic Community of West African States.

There are 110 ECOMOG troops, mostly from Togo, in the country as part of the peace accord. Hundreds more were due to arrive this week.

A French navy ship with 300 ECOMOG peacekeepers on board was unable to dock in Bissau due to the shelling, Lusa reported.

The peacekeeping force was to act as a buffer between the breakaway military faction and the mostly Senegalese troops supporting President Joao Bernardo Vieira.

Most of the country's 6,000-strong army have joined the rebellion aimed at deposing Veira. The insurgents say Vieira is corrupt.

According to its per-capita income, Guinea-Bissau is one of the 15 poorest nations in the world.

-30-

e. Mir

BY ANNA DOLGOV
THE ASSOCIATED PRESS

MOSCOW — A large spaced mirror, billed as a prototype for giant reflectors that would send sunlight to Arctic cities during dark winters, failed to unfurl yesterday. Frustrated Russian scientists vowed to try again today.

As a small Russian cargo ship orbited more than 200 miles above Earth, the glistening metallic membranes of the 83-foot collapsible mirror began unfolding as planned. But the petal-shaped panels appeared to snag on the cargo ship's antenna, and the structure was stuck half-folded.

One of the most spectacular experiments ever staged by Russian Mir cosmonauts was later called off, and scientists scrambled to find a solution for another try.

The mirror was to have worked like an artificial moon, reflecting sunlight onto several regions in Russia and other former Soviet republics, Europe, Canada, and South Dakota.

Space experts hoped it would serve as a prototype for 650-foot models that could illuminate sun-starved cities, cutting through long winter nights to shine light on regions that do not see much of the sun for months.

Had the experiment gone smoothly, the mirror would have shone light on a spot about five miles in diameter, provided the sky was clear, said Valery Lyndin, a Mission Control spokesman.

Mir cosmonauts Gennady Padalka and Sergei Avdeyev started the experiment yesterday afternoon by jettisoning the Progress cargo ship, with the folded mirror attached, from the station.

They then sent a remote command to unfold the mirror. As the mirror rotated, a system of weights and strings began to pull the panels open.

But within minutes, the mirror became stuck.

-30-

Chapter 9

After the fact: Editing features and more complex story structures

Feature copy sometimes provides a welcome respite from the hard-news stories on disasters, crime and politics — for editors and readers alike. Yet these stories, and their headlines, also demand a special finesse. That's why the copy-desk chief often will assign the most talented, experienced staffers to handle these "plums."

It's important, as with any story, to catch any mechanical and/or factual errors. But sometimes, the "looser" style of feature writing includes deliberate deviations from news style and even standard English. A well-placed sentence fragment, for example, may be intentionally used for effect. And feature stories usually don't begin with a who-what-where-when summary lead; feature writers often use techniques such as anecdotes, scene-setting and flashbacks, which you're used to seeing in fiction writing.

So, whereas you must remain vigilant to ensure clarity and accuracy in these stories, you may find you need to use a lighter touch in editing to preserve the writer's style.

Exercises

1. Find a story in your local newspaper, written in "straight" news style that you think could be rewritten as a feature. Rewrite the lead, using a technique other than a summary lead.

2. Edit the following feature stories according to your instructor's directions:

   a. Pinned

   BY MARK DAVIS
   PHILADELPHIA INQUIRER STAFF WRITER

   In that moment before people yelled and sirens sounded, when Lisa Desmarets was convinced that she and her unborn child would die under the big tree that fell on her in Monday's wind and rain storm, she closed her eyes.

   Hail Mary, she began, mouthing the words she had learned as a child, *full of grace ...*

Then someone yelled, and Desmarets, 19 and eight months' pregnant, heard the pounding feet of people running toward the spot in South Philadelphia where she lay under a 60-foot oak toppled by high winds. Moments later, an ambulance whooped in the distance.

"I thought I was going to die under that tree," Desmarets said yesterday as she rested at the Hospital of the University of Pennsylvania, where she was listed in fair condition. "I can't believe I'm doing as good as I am, after having a tree fall on me."

Good fortune or bad luck? Maybe both descriptions fit what happened to Desmarets.

About 4:25 p.m. Monday, as an unexpected, fierce windstorm began forming in the region, Desmarets and her fiance, Jeffery Putnam, stepped out of their home near 19th and McKean Streets. With them was their dog, Scoobie-Doo, a collie-greyhound mix.

The day was breezy and overcast as they headed toward Marconi Plaza to walk the dog.

As they made the 15-minute walk to the park at Broad Street and Oregon Avenue, they watched the sky. "It went from gray to green and back to gray," she said. "It looked really freaky."

The sudden storm swept across the region, delaying SEPTA trains, downing power lines, and ripping off roofs. National Weather Service officials examined the site of the damage yesterday and said a tornado had touched down.

In South Philadelphia, the occasional breezes that greeted the two pedestrians became a wind, that gusted up to 70 m.p.h. and howled and yanked at their coats. Tree limbs clattered overhead. Streetlights bobbed. Desmarets, only a month from delivery, struggled to walk upright.

A gust pushed her in the back, and she pitched forward, landing on the sidewalk.

Then — *craaack!* An oak, the last in a line of giants that shade the park in the summer, swayed and bent. Then it broke.

Desmarets rolled onto her right side, looking toward the sky. She had only enough time to close her eyes.

Crash! Dirt flew and branches snapped as the tree thundered to the ground.

Then, stillness. Desmarets opened her eyes. She was under the trunk, curled in the fork formed by two large limbs, with one branch shoved against her left side and the second barely clearing her head. She wiggled her body once, twice; the tree didn't move. Then she tried moving her legs; they wriggled against earth and wood, stuck.

Everywhere she looked, Desmarets said, all she could see was the tree that had entombed her in its wooden cage. Nearby, another oak tree had fallen — proof of the storm's sudden ferocity. "It was like I was under a tent," she said. "I felt like I was stuck in a dome."

Putnam took off his coat, folded it, and slid it under her head, urging his fiancee to be brave. Somebody dialed 911. Within minutes, a Fire Department rescue crew was working on the tree, slowly lifting it with heavy-duty, inflatable balloons and sliding pieces of wood under the trunk as it got higher.

She was free in 20 minutes. As rescue workers hustled her to the ambulance, Desmarets heard a new sound — the sputter of a chain saw.

Desmarets suffered a fractured pelvis and lacerations and was in serious condition when she arrived at the hospital. Her injuries should not interfere with the birth of her child, which a sonogram yesterday revealed to be a boy, hospital officials said.

"We get trauma cases in here, but at this time of the year, it's usually people slipping on the ice," said Peter Argenta, the hospital's chief of obstetrics and gynecology. "I think this is the first time we've seen anything like this."

And Desmarets? "I guess I'm pretty lucky," she said.

A little impatient, too. She has a story she can't wait to tell her son.

-30-

b. Online romance

BY MARGIE BOULÉ
THE OREGONIAN

Most of the time when you see Clatsop County District Attorney Josh Marquis in the media, he's talking about how many times a victim was stabbed or explaining exactly how a husband pushed his wife over a cliff.

By the same token, when Cindy Price's name is in the media, most often she's in Europe at some kind of NATO policy conference, and she's the reporter. Or she's on KMUN Radio in Astoria, discussing cultural affairs.

But this week, Josh and Cindy are featured in People magazine. This week Josh and Cindy are media stars because of Love.

"Like 'You've Got Mail's' cybersweeties," begins the magazine story, "these couples met on the Net — then turned online romance into a real-world walk down the aisle." Which makes it sound like Josh and Cindy signed on to AOL looking for love. Which makes Josh crazy.

"Josh always says we didn't meet online," Cindy says.

"The point I try to stress," Josh says, "is that we met at a dinner party that was the result of things we'd written online."

"But I like to give more credit to AOL and the online universe," Cindy says. "The smart part of the online universe. Not the romance rooms."

Most folks would not call Josh and Cindy's meeting romantic. They did, after all, become aware of each other in 1995, in a Court TV message group that discussed the O.J. Simpson case on America Online. Not your most romantic setting.

Still, most of the contributors were intelligent people, making thoughtful points. As a prosecutor, Josh was fascinated by the case. He posted messages regularly.

"So I knew a lot about 'CoastDA' (Josh's online) before I met him," says Cindy, who was living in Los Angeles then. "I knew he was a witty guy, and smart. He would write about big issues and put in great references to movies and music."

Josh noticed Cindy, too. "The first thing was her sense of humor," Josh says. "She was sharp and funny. In our group of maybe 40 people, some were predictable, some kind of goofy, some pedantic. Cindy's writing was crisp and to the point."

In the fall of 1995 someone suggested the group meet in L.A. And that's how Josh and Cindy came to lay eyes on each other on Oct. 28, 1995, at the Beverly Hills Tennis Club.

Though both were single, neither had been looking for love in the O.J. chat room. Cindy, long divorced, was wary about another relationship. Josh, who'd never been married, was immersed in his new job as Clatsop County district attorney. In fact, Josh, who was visiting his folks in L.A., almost didn't attend. "I'm not much of a social animal outside of politics," he says. "I kind of swallowed before I went in. I thought, well, I'm here. I might as well do it."

Josh was standing out by the pool when Cindy arrived. "I'll never forget walking in," Cindy says. "I was looking forward to meeting some people who'd entertained me . . . over the months. I asked, 'Is 'Seaotter' here? Is 'CoastDA' here?' The only one there was 'CoastDA.' He had his back to me." And here we must be honest: If Cindy hadn't already read a lot of Josh's thoughts online, "I never would have paid attention to him. He looked too professorial." (Josh's father is a professor. He must have inherited the look.) "And I never would have gone for a DA. I've rebelled against authority my whole life. His hair was too short, his pants too long. I was still into saxophone players. What can I tell you?"

That was about to change. Cindy touched Josh's arm and said, "Hi. I'm 'Deanadolar.' " And that was it, they agree. Josh saw a "really pretty" woman. And the "professor" who turned to meet Cindy was, she says, "an attractive guy, taller, with this nice build, nice smile. And a great talker."

Josh evidently became a social animal that day because the two talked all evening. There followed what Cindy describes as "a whirlwind three months of massive phone bills and massive e-mails." She has a red three-ring binder with all 500 messages sent between Oct. 28 and the end of 1995.

Josh arranged for Cindy to stay at an Astoria bed and breakfast on her first visit; he made trips south and stayed with his folks. And they fell in love. Soon they were flying north and south every chance they got. And then they met for a vacation in Europe. "Originally, Cindy wanted to go to Bosnia," Josh says, laughing. "I said absolutely not. They were still shooting then! She said she could arrange for a U.N. escort." They went to Venice and Slovenia instead.

But any woman who wanted to vacation in Bosnia was the right wife for a man who prosecutes accused murderers for a living. They married in July 1996.

Cindy moved to Astoria. She still works as a free-lance writer and editor. But home is in Oregon. They're happy. Josh isn't shy about telling people how much he loves his wife. And Cindy says her life is "exquisitely better than it ever was. My only regret is I didn't meet Josh 20 years sooner. Mainly because two months after I moved here, I heard on the radio that Oregon just entered a 20-year wet cycle." There's that humor Josh noticed so early. "But really," she says, "almost all my dreams have come true."

-30-

c. South

BY SUE ANNE PRESSLEY
WASHINGTON POST STAFF WRITER

HARDEEVILLE, S.C. — Henry Ingram does not cotton to Yankees. He has, in fact, taken legal steps at the Jasper County Courthouse here to ensure that no Yankee can ever trespass on or purchase his Delta Plantation, a 1,700-acre abandoned rice farm filled with water turkeys, snowy egrets, moss-draped oaks, slave-built roads and the ghosts of Sherman's march to the sea.

"Yankees just don't know how to act," grumbled Ingram, 60, a firecracker and video poker tycoon who recently ran for mayor of the nearby resort town of Hilton Head Island with a tongue-in-cheek suggestion that Yankee transplants receive a one-way bus ticket home. "We didn't have any trouble until they started coming down here, telling us how to do things."

His is one southerner's reaction, admittedly extreme, to living in an area that is changing so dramatically — growing faster than any other region in the United States — that it no longer resembles the South of his youth — or even, for that matter, the South of the 1980s. But Ingram, as he knows, is fighting a losing cause. The South — here in the coastlands north of Savannah, Ga., and across broad swaths of the former Confederacy — in large part already is slipping out of the grasp of people considered traditional southerners.

As the region becomes more diverse and more in sync with the rest of the nation, spurred by a better-educated middle class and a vibrant, more egalitarian economy, it also appears to be forfeiting some of the distinctive qualities that always made it such a reliable stereotype — the butt of jokes and the darling of songwriters and novelists.

In more and more places in the 14 states that make up the South, people no longer know who their neighbors are. They no longer live mainly on farms and in the country; seven of 10 southerners now live in metropolitan areas, according to a recent study. They are no longer just black and white, either; Hispanics, migrating beyond Texas and Florida, make up 11 percent of the population, and the number of Asians, although smaller, has increased more than 48 percent during the 1990s alone.

And instead of people fleeing the South, as whites did during the Great Depression in search of a better way of life, and as blacks did during post-World War II in search of more equal opportunities, newcomers now are flocking here in unprecedented droves. From the Northeast, from the Midwest, even from California, they are streaming in, at a steady rate of a million a year, drawn by jobs, mild weather, a new emphasis on public and higher education and a still-affordable lifestyle that remains relatively relaxed.

They are making the southern accent almost endangered — and prompting diehards such as Ingram to broaden their definition of Yankee. Indeed, the depopulation trend has been so fully reversed that one in three Americans — or 87 million people — call the South home.

"This is a section of the country that was insulated for 200 years by its own poverty and discrimination, and the earlier waves of immigration that rolled over the rest of the country just didn't happen here," said George Autry, president of MDC Inc., a Chapel Hill, N.C., think tank that has tracked the region's economic development for 30 years and whose recent report, "The State of the South," delineated the changes. "We have been insulated. And now we're the part of the country that is experiencing the most in-migration."

No region in the nation is debated as passionately as the South, and no region carries more baggage from the past, the legacy of slavery and the later Jim Crow policies. More than 130 years after the final defeat at Appomattox, the Civil War still reverberates; Ingram, for one, speaks of the "war of northern aggression" as if it took place yesterday. Regional icons of that era — the Confederate flag, still flying daily outside the South Carolina Capitol; the song "Dixie" still sung at the Citadel and many other places — persist despite efforts by certain groups to remove them as symbols of racism.

But with that rebel pride there also has been a corresponding awareness that the rest of the world often viewed the southerner as backward, insular, lackadaisical about education and possessed of a religiosity so consuming that outsiders often saw it as either dictatorial or comical. For decades, southerners assumed America was made up of themselves, and everyone else — who did not understand or care to embrace the South's peculiarities. And that is what is being "all shook up," as "The State of the South" report puts it, by the increasing variety and continuing shifts in the region's population.

The old order of the South, it seems, has become disordered.

The impact is notable in the largest cities — such as Atlanta and Charlotte, both booming during the 1990s — but also is being felt in the smaller, less obvious towns, especially in the Carolinas and Georgia.

Hilton Head Island, S.C., once valued chiefly for its sea pine timber and incorporated only since 1983, now has 30,000 largely well-heeled newcomers, and the blacks who serve its hotels and resorts are bused in from the countryside.

Cary, N.C., in the high-tech Research Triangle area near Raleigh, has exploded from a 1990 population of not quite 45,000 to 85,000 a mere eight years later, with 50 percent of adult residents possessing a college degree. A common joke is that the town's name now rightly stands for "Corral Area for Relocated Yankees."

Although the influx of newcomers grates on many old-timers' nerves, other longtime residents describe the growth as a good thing.

"In the old days, this was a one-stoplight town, and it was right outside my drugstore," said Cary pharmacist Ralph Ashworth, who has been in business there for 42 years. "Then IBM came in 1960, and people have been coming ever since. Frankly, I've always considered it a plus to have the diversity of new people — they've brought new ideas and a lot of the cultural things we probably wouldn't have had otherwise. Of course, you're always going to have some people who don't like change. They like the status quo. You hear them complain, 'The road goes both ways.'"

In Hickory, N.C., a town of 30,000 on the edge of the Blue Ridge Mountains, the furniture and hosiery factories that once provided blue-collar whites with stable jobs are seeking out Asian and Hispanic immigrants who also are enrolled in community college programs to learn better English. At a time when the area's unemployment rate is a scant 3 percent, the emergence of this new work force is creating few tensions, a situation that could change rapidly if a real competition for unskilled jobs sets in again.

Not every part of the South, however, is undergoing a transformation. Kentucky is lagging in overall growth, as are Arkansas, Louisiana, Mississippi and West Virginia. Venture into isolated sections of northeastern North Carolina, and "they look more like they did when Sir Walter Raleigh sent his parties ashore," Autry said, despite an overall gain of nearly a half-million new residents in the state this decade.

And the specter of southern poverty has hardly been obliterated. A recent report by the Children's Defense Fund pointed out that one-fourth (or 5.5 million) of southern children remain poor, and that 84 of the nation's 100 poorest counties for children are in the South. The difference is that now, according to U.S. Census figures, 1 million of those poor Southern children are Hispanic.

But the story of this newly minted South is, for now, much more a story of prosperity. Nowhere is this more obvious than in the fastest-growing area of South Carolina — Hilton Head Island. Shaped like a running shoe, the barrier isle 30 miles north of Savannah and 90 miles south of Charleston attracts 2.38 million tourists a year to its 3,000 hotel rooms, 1,000 time-share units, 23 golf courses, 300 tennis courts, eight marinas, 36 shopping areas and 236 restaurants. Today's Hilton Head is light years removed from the isolated enclave of fishermen, lumbermen, and descendants of freed slaves, speaking their own Gullah dialect, who forged its past.

Although the area has a well-documented reputation as a haven for older residents — nearly half are older than 45, and a Sun City retirement community with an eventual 8,000 new homes is going up in nearby Bluffton — it also has begun to attract younger families, such as the Schonings, formerly of Summit, N.J. Pete and Kim moved here three years ago with their two young daughters, followed in short order by Kim's parents, her sister and niece.

"The weather in New Jersey just didn't cooperate that much," said Kim Schoning, 36, "and we wanted to raise our kids in a nice area."

What sort of South will emerge from all of these newcomers, all of these changes — indeed, whether the South is dying — is a subject that may always fascinate southerners, who love to contemplate such things. As Henry Ingram appears regularly on radio talk shows to air his anti-Yankee sentiments, neo-Confederate groups are arising to "preserve the orthodox conservative Christian culture of the South against all the forces of modernity," said Michael Hill, a founder of the League of the South.

"Southerners are still a distinctive and definable folk," said Hill, a historian Tillman College in Tuscaloosa, Ala., "and the league encourages them to stand up and say, 'If you don't like the way we do things down here, Delta is ready when you are.'"

John Shelton Reed, director of the Institute for Research and Social Science at the University of North Carolina, and Hodding Carter III, the Mississippi newspaperman who was State Department spokesman during the Carter administration, have made entertainment out of their periodic duels about whether the South is being Americanized or America is being southernized..

Reed, who also co-edits a new quarterly called Southern Cultures, takes the position that "it's easy to overstate the changes taking place — much of the South and most of its people have been bypassed." Carter makes the point that newcomers, as much as anyone, cherish the myth of the South. An attempt to change the name of the Dixie Living section of the Atlanta Journal-Constitution a few years ago provoked a huge outcry, Carter said, largely from former midwesterners "who protested that that's what they came here for — the southern mystique."

In politics, Carter said, middle-class southern whites have simply begun to vote as the middle classes elsewhere in America often have — as Republicans, looking out for their own economic interests. But when it comes to God and Jesus, the old-time religion of the South has expanded far beyond its borders to the rest of America, as a reaction perhaps to the stress of modern times.

George Autry, of MDC Inc., maintains that there is nothing really to worry about; there will always be a South. "Can you imagine a 'State of the North' report? Can you imagine 'Northern Cultures'? That's an oxymoron. The North is not really a place, it's a direction."

Even Henry Ingram is not feeling so threatened that he won't make allowances for a rehabilitated Yankee. All one has to do is take his "southern oath," which pledges, in part, to "love and honor the true southern way of life" and to "never mention the word Sherman unless it is to describe his cowardly and inhuman characteristics."

The final requirement for the former Yankee is to whistle "Dixie" as "a token of my new outlook on life."

-30-

CHAPTER 10

No safety in numbers: Polls and survey stories

Be honest: Many of you went into journalism because you were allergic to any discipline involving heavy-duty math. But numbers crop up everywhere — in stories about the municipal budget, crime, education, business and science, and in the ubiquitous reports on public-opinion polls.

Polls help you keep your fingers on the readers' and viewers' pulse. If well conducted, polls provide insights into trends in public opinion and concerns. As an editor, however, you must be aware of some pitfalls in reports on polls and surveys. You need to consider the source of any poll and evaluate its validity in terms of how it was conducted. Ask yourself how large was the sample of people polled. How were they chosen? When and how were they questioned (by mail, phone, in person)?

For example, in a person-on-the-street "survey," five or six people are chosen "randomly" and interviewed on a question of the day. This is not a scientific poll and should not be overrepresented as any indication of broader public opinion. Its only real value is entertainment, so only the most colorful or insightful quotes should be used.

Another potential pitfall is the sponsor of the poll. Your antennae should automatically go up if you see that the poll was conducted by an organization with a vested interest in the outcome. That doesn't necessarily mean holding the story, but you definitely should include information on the sponsor so the audience can take that into account. You also should provide the audience with the exact wording of questions, perhaps in a sidebar that gives other information about how the poll was conducted.

A story for a general-audience publication shouldn't get bogged down in the jargon and technicalities of polling, but as an editor, you do need to familiarize yourself with certain terms, such as "margin of error," so you can evaluate and explain a poll.

Finally, you need to double-check any math and percentages used, and make sure to follow the correct style for numbers.

Public Agenda, a nonpartisan, nonprofit research organization, analyzes public opinion drawn from all the major polls and also offers advice on avoiding pitfalls in interpreting polls. You might want to check out its Web site: <www.publicagenda.org>.

The following exercises are designed to help you brush up on some basic math and get some practice in handling stories based on polls and surveys.

Exercises

1. Circle the correct answer(s) or fill in the blank:

   a. If a mayoral candidate wins an election by a vote of 30,000 to 15,000, his victory is by a [margin / ratio] of [two to one / 2-1].

   b. Find 25 percent of 80, and show the steps you used to calculate the answer.

   c. 75 is _____ percent of 90.

   d. 35 percent of _____ is 8.4.

   e. A shoe store advertises a sale in which certain brands are marked down 15 percent. What would the sale price be on a pair of shoes regularly priced at $79?

   f. If the rate of return on a particular investment falls from 10 percent to 8 percent, the decline is 2 [percent / percentage points / Either is correct].

   g. If a town's population grows from 10,526 to 12,711, it increases _____ percent.

   h. If student enrollment at a university falls from 25,743 to 24,865, it declines _____ percent.

   i. If an organization reduces its $450,000 annual budget by 3 percent, the new budget total is _____.

   j. The latest election poll indicates Candidate A is leading, with 55 percent of likely voters' support, compared with 45 percent for Candidate B. This poll has a margin of error of plus or minus 6 percentage points. What can you deduce from this poll about the likely outcome of the race?

2. Find an example of a report on a survey or poll in a newspaper, magazine or other publication. Who conducted the poll? When and how? How many respondents were included, and how were they chosen? If you were editing a story about this poll, what further information would you seek from the reporter?

3. Edit the following stories according to directions from your instructor, and make a note of any missing or incomplete information.

a. Business

BY HARRY ZIMBLER
REGIONAL BUSINESS ANALYST, PENNSYLVANIA BUSINESS CENTRAL

HARRISBURG, Pa. — The Eighth Annual Pennsylvania Economic Survey demonstrates continued optimism among the Commonwealth's business leaders.

Commissioned by the Pennsylvania Chamber of Business & Industry and administered by PriceWaterhouseCoopers, the survey measures the attitudes and opinions of the state's business leaders. The survey, conducted last July 1998, does not reflect any reactions to the market downturn in August and September, or the deepening problems in the Asian economies.

The survey was mailed to 3,632 chamber members. This year, 604 business leaders returned the survey, representing a return of 15.8 percent. The chamber believes that the results offer a good snapshot of what is on the minds of business leaders.

In general, the survey clearly demonstrates that business leaders are happy with the general direction of the state's economy. Sixty-three percent of the respondents believe the state's economy has grown in the past 12 months, a ten percent increase from 1997's report. A record low — only 10.1 percent of all respondents — felt the economy declined in the past year.

In nearly every category, actual economic growth exceeded the 1997 predictions of the respondents. For example, while 50 percent of the business leaders participating in the 1997 predicted economic growth for 1998, 60 percent actually achieved growth in the year measured.

The employment outlook appears bright, considering the fact that nearly 42 percent of the respondents plan to add employees over the next year, a 2.9 percent over last year's results. Actual employment in Pennsylvania has increased by more than 230,000 since 1995.

Reducing business taxes continues to be the top issue among business leaders, despite the Ridge administration's successful efforts to reduce taxes. This topic has held the top spot for four of the last six years. Other important business issues include workers' compensation and environmental policy. PriceWaterhouseCoopers believes that many respondents are waiting to see if recent business tax reductions will have the impact that was predicted for them.

A profile of the leaders reveals that 45.2 percent work in the manufacturing sector. The service sector is next (22.5 percent), with wholesale trade third (7.5 percent).

Company size was ranked by sales volume. The majority of respondents — 52.1 percent — were from organizations that had between $1 million and $15 million in sales, while 38.6 percent of the companies employed between 25 and 99 people.

For the first time ever, businesses from central Pennsylvania accounted for more than half of the responses to the survey. Both the western and eastern regions continue to decline in size, although more than twice as many eastern companies as western companies responded.

Service industry representatives expressed the greatest level of optimism, with more than 50 percent of surveys indicating plans to add workers in 1999. The construction sector ranked second at 48.9 percent, with manufacturing third. Interestingly, 72.7 percent of the manufacturing respondents experienced growth in 1998, although only 42.5 percent plan to add to their workforce.

The respondents continue to view Pennsylvania's business climate more favorably, despite their ongoing concerns about business taxes. Nearly 59 percent rate the overall climate as good to excellent for business.

For the past three years the number of businesses seriously considering relocating outside of Pennsylvania has decreased. In 1998, only 24 percent would do so. Not surprisingly, the top worries of companies that would consider moving out of Pennsylvania mirrored the concerns of the general universe of the survey. Why would a business consider packing up and moving away? Business taxes, workers' compensation, and the need for a better labor force are all on the minds of Pennsylvania's business leaders.

According to PriceWaterhouseCoopers, the full advantages of a $1.2 billion reduction in Pennsylvania's business taxes may not yet be measured. Today, Pennsylvania ranks tenth in the nation for the creation of new manufacturing facilities, and tenth in new manufacturing businesses. There are 32 Fortune 500 companies and 42 Forbes 500 companies located in the Commonwealth.

-30-

b. Sex

BY JOHN SCHWARTZ
WASHINGTON POST

A surprisingly large number of American men and women are unlucky in love — or at least, in sex — according to the first study to explore the full range of sexual problems of men and women in the general population since the Kinsey reports of a half-century ago.

Four out of 10 women and nearly one-third of men suffer from a variety of problems in the bedroom grouped under the general heading "sexual dysfunction," according to the new study. The list includes lack of sexual desire, physical pain during intercourse, an inability to become sexually aroused or to complete sexual acts, premature climax, and anxiety about sexual performance.

"The rates are far higher than anyone had really anticipated," said Edward Laumann, a sociology professor at the University of Chicago and lead author of the study. Yet if anything, the prevalence of sexual problems is somewhat higher than the survey findings indicate, Laumann said. "You don't really expect people to rush up and tell people they're impotent."

More important, Laumann said, most people who experience sexual difficulties do not seek help from doctors or sexual educators — only one in 10 men and as few as one in seven women — so "the iceberg effect here is really enormous," and could help to explain last year's hoopla over the impotence drug Viagra.*

"With the strong association between sexual dysfunction and impaired quality of life, this problem warrants recognition as a significant public health concern," concluded the authors, whose work appears in the issue of the Journal of the American Medical Association published today.

Men and women go through sexual difficulties at different stages of their lives, the study shows. Women tend to have problems in youth, with 21 percent of women between the ages of 18 and 29 reporting physical pain during intercourse. Women between the ages of 50 and 59 were one-third as likely to say that they had experienced pain during sex.

Men's problems, by contrast, grow more pronounced with age, with men in the 50-to-59-year-old age group 3 1/2 times more likely to have problems getting and maintaining an erection than men in the 18- to 25-year-old group.

Married men and women appear to have fewer sexual problems than singles. And education, too, was linked to sexual satisfaction, with women who did not complete high school nearly twice as likely to report lack of sexual desire (42 percent) as college-educated women (24 percent). Men who completed college also were less likely to report premature climax than those who did not graduate from high school — 27 percent vs. 38 percent.

The researchers said they were impressed with the close association between stress and sexual problems. Falling income was linked to trouble in the bedroom, and men who lost their jobs tended to encounter trouble getting and maintaining an erection, Laumann said. Health problems correlated with low sexual satisfaction, and so did sexual abuse in childhood.

In fact, people reporting sexual dysfunction were less likely to report general feelings of happiness than those enjoying better sexual relations — though the researchers cautioned that it was unclear whether the sexual problems caused the unhappiness or vice versa. The only measure of sexual dysfunction that was not associated with a report of lower quality of life were men with premature ejaculation.

The only similar attempt to assess sexual practices among such a broad cross-section of the population was conducted by biologist Alfred Charles Kinsey, whose research into the sexual habits of thousands of men and women in the 1940s and '50s revolutionized American sexual mores, making sex and its many permutations a part of the national conversation. Kinsey has since come under attack for some of his methods and subjects.

The new study was based on data from the 1992 National Health and Social Life Survey, a comprehensive research effort involving 90-minute, face-to-face interviews with 1,749 women and 1,410 men — enough, the researchers estimate, to be a representative sample of 97 percent of the nation. Because the results come from a single survey, they cannot show whether the rates of sexual dysfunction are on the rise or are waning. An earlier report drawn from the survey, published in 1994, focused on American sexual practices.

-30-

* A day after this story ran, the Associated Press reported an acknowledgment from the American Medical Association that its journal had failed to disclose that the maker of Viagra, Pfizer Inc., had paid the sex-study authors for earlier work. A spokesman for the Journal of the American Medical Association said the authors disclosed that Pfizer had paid them to review clinical trial data on Viagra before the drug was submitted for government approval. He said it was an oversight that JAMA editors did not include this information in the sex-study report.

c. Health

BY WILL LESTER
THE ASSOCIATED PRESS

WASHINGTON — Americans are generally happy with their health insurance coverage, but four in 10 adults say insurers have a bigger say than doctors in the care they receive, according to a new poll.

Women are more critical than men, with 40 percent saying the health care system is in worse shape than it was five years ago, says the poll conducted for The Associated Press. The biggest complaint was the inability of people to choose their own doctor.

As these concerns grow, Congress is again considering how to give people more control over their own health care without substantially increasing costs.

Nine out of 10 Americans said they were very satisfied or somewhat satisfied with their health insurance coverage, the survey found.

But among those with concerns about health care, much of that dissatisfaction is centered around the growing loss of control people feel over their medical care, an intensely personal issue.

The poll of 1,008 people taken Jan. 29 through Tuesday was done by ICR of Media, Pa.

Making some changes in the system sounds like a good idea to Thomas Feagley, a 42-year-old father of three, whose health plan required him to change family doctors last year.

"There needs to be an investigation or some kind of fine tuning," said the custodian of athletic fields at schools near Huntingdon, Pa., who used the team doctor as his family physician for years. "I would have been a happy camper if I could have gotten my insurance and kept my doctor."

The growing loss of personal control over health care has left Feagley uneasy about the future. He changed doctors a year ago and now that doctor is leaving his practice.

When people were asked their biggest concern about health care, the most-mentioned complaint was limits on their ability to pick the doctor of their choice, cited by 28 percent, followed by concerns about cost and quality.

"I know they have to have guidelines," Feagley said, but he noted his former doctor treats many others in his family. "We had kind of a family thing going on."

-30-

CHAPTER 11

Doing justice: Legal issues, ethics and bias

Legal issues have been and will continue to be important considerations for publications and those who work on them. With juries returning verdicts in excess of $200 million against such august newspapers as The Wall Street Journal, the need to make sure your publication is not successfully sued is of the utmost importance. But even an unsuccessful lawsuit can be costly to defend.

Stories about people suing the media appear in the press with regularity. By far the greatest threat to the media is the prospect of a libel suit. *Libel* is the legal term for making a false and defamatory statement in print about a person or a company. *Defamation* means making others think less of you or causing them to shun or avoid you. People are defamed every day when one says truthful things about them that also hurt their reputations. But for a lawsuit to be successful, the defamatory statement also needs to be false. In addition, successful libel suits must also show that the defamatory statement was published (which is assumed for the mass media), that the person was identifiable (even if a name was not used), and that the publication was at fault. The last requirement is the most complicated, but, in brief, it means that if a person is a public official, public figure or someone who involved himself or herself in a public controversy, then to win a libel suit, that person must be able to prove that the publisher had knowledge that what was published was false or exhibited a reckless disregard for whether it was false. This is known as the "actual malice" standard. For private individuals in most states the "fault" standard is negligence, a much easier level of fault to prove.

There are several defenses to a libel suit, but among the most commonly used are truth, privilege and opinion. *Truth* is an ironclad defense, and the burden is generally on the plaintiff to prove the alleged libel was false. *Privilege* usually means that the statement was said in some official and protected context, such as a courtroom. Reporting such a privileged statement is also protected as long as the report is fair and accurate. *Opinion* is more complex, but as long as the facts underlying the statements of opinion are revealed or well known, then stating an opinion is protected.

Privacy issues also are a growing concern. Privacy law is divided into four separate torts: appropriation, intrusion, publicity about private facts and false light. Each is a distinct area of law and may be treated differently in different jurisdictions. Indeed, false light, for example, is not even recognized in some states. What this means is that you will need to become familiar with the law of your state; only the most general aspects of law can be dealt with in this chapter.

Briefly, *appropriation* is the use of someone's image or likeness for trade or commercial purposes without his or her permission. This sometimes happens when a famous person's picture is used in an ad. *Intrusion* is the invasion of someone's expectation of solitude. The media most often seem to get in trouble with intrusion when they go on someone's property without the owner's permission. This is the civil equivalent of criminal trespass and can occur regardless of whether a story is printed. *Publicity about private facts* is the publicizing of information about someone that would be highly offensive to a reasonable person and not of legitimate public concern. The press occasionally is accused of doing this when stories are run recounting a notorious crime from the past. But, in general, courts have not found these kinds of stories to be offensive and not of legitimate public concern. Finally, *false light* turns libel on its head by making publication of false but *not* defamatory information actionable if such publication portrays a person in a false light that would be offensive to a reasonable person and if the publisher is at fault, as in libel.

Obviously, in this brief review of libel and privacy law it is impossible to go into the nuances of the thousands of cases that have shaped and refined the case law. If you have questions about a particular story, you should consult an attorney.

Ethical questions are similar to legal questions in that issues are often very nearly the same, but the consequences of an ethical lapse may not be quite as financially draining as is the case in legal lapses. *Ethics* has to do with what a person *ought* to do, covering the gray area between what is not legal and what is not only legal but something that you wouldn't mind becoming public knowledge. One test of ethical appropriateness, then, is the level of embarrassment that would be caused if the process that led to a decision to publish were completely open to public scrutiny. And, indeed, it is sometimes the fact that when errors do occur, the way that they are dealt with after the fact has a lot to do with the public acceptance of a newspaper's actions. This happened, for example, in 1981 with the Washington Post's Janet Cooke. She was a reporter who fabricated stories about a 7-year-old heroin addict. The stories were so compelling that Cooke won a Pulitzer Prize for them. But shortly after she received the award she confessed that she had made up the stories. She returned the Pulitzer Prize and was fired. The Post devoted many columns to examining and explaining to readers how a reporter could pass off stories as factual, fooling a phalanx of editors. Performing this public act of penance helped readers regain the trust they had placed in the Post, but for many years afterward this case was held up as an aberration in journalistic integrity.

Most ethical lapses are not as egregious as Janet Cooke's (although the summer of 1998 found writer Stephen Glass acknowledging that he made up stories that were published in reputable magazines. Also, Boston Globe columnists Patricia Smith and Mike Barnicle resigned after it was shown that they had fabricated stories and plagiarized). But ethical questions do come up regularly. In November 1997, Bobbi McCaughey gave birth to septuplets. She and her husband were pictured on the covers of both Time and Newsweek; however, Newsweek lightened, brightened and straightened Mrs. McCaughey's teeth. Time, it was clear to see, made no such alteration. How did Newsweek publicly justify its manipulation of the image? "The editors decided to lighten and improve the picture. In the process of doing that the technical people went too far. The mistake was in guessing what was in the shadow and changing it." That explanation might have been satisfactory except that three years earlier Time had darkened an official police mug shot of O.J. Simpson to use as its cover illustration. Newsweek used the same picture but did not change the tones. There was public speculation as to Time's intent in making Simpson look more sinister. Now the shoe was on the other foot. Altering images is one of the most troubling ethical issues in journalism, and even the most reputable publications can succumb to the temptation, as National Geographic once did when it moved the Egyptian pyramids in one of its cover shots.

Consider the issue of lying to get a great story. Is the greater good served by using deceptive tactics to get a story, as ABC News did when two of its employees went undercover to expose unsanitary conditions? What about using stolen government secrets to reveal the true extent of United States involvement in a war, as The New York Times did with the Pentagon Papers? Are the consequences more important than the tactics? What about prying into the private lives of politicians? What if they invite such scrutiny, as Gary Hart did when he ran for president?

One test of all such ethical questions is whether they can stand up to public and professional scrutiny. If nothing else, such public debates help us all decide individually — if not collectively — what is acceptable professional behavior. Without such debates, it is difficult to know whether you have crossed an invisible line until it is too late. In an op-ed column in The Washington Post in 1998, after a series of ethical problems in journalism came to light, Richard Harwood quoted Norman Isaacs: "What we need are not reporters' newspapers but readers' newspapers — and what it takes to create them is good editing."

Exercises

1. Scan some newspapers for stories about lawsuits against the press. They appear with some regularity in the "People" section. If these are difficult to find, use an online database to search for stories with key words such as *libel, sue* and *defame*. Share these stories with classmates, and discuss why the suit was brought and what the copy editor could have done to reduce the chance that the person would sue the newspaper.

2. *The Associated Press Stylebook and Libel Manual* lists a number of defenses in a libel suit: truth, privilege, and fair comment and criticism. Also important are the distinctions between public officials and public figures and private figures. How, if at all, do or should these defenses affect the way a story is written and edited?

3. Although it is legal to run the name of a rape victim, just as it is to run the name of a carjacking victim, many news organizations do not. Discuss the ethical pros and cons of running the names of the victims of sex crimes.

4. Consider the following story:

    A group of African American men from out of state visited the campus of State U., a historically black state university. The group went to a dorm looking for women, and a fight between the out-of-towners and a group of State U. students erupted. Police arrested the out-of-towners, but a student mob stormed the campus security office where the out-of-towners were being held and more violence ensued. In a follow-up column several days after the event, the region's largest newspaper, The Tattler, described the incident, focusing on the fact that both the out-of-towners and the State U. students were African Americans. It also discussed the school's attempt to minimize the role its students played in the incident. The column went on:

    > Writing to a local newspaper, university President Samuel Smith questioned remarks by the district attorney that one of the out-of-towners had been stabbed. When District Attorney Jeremiah J. Jones III replied by quoting from police reports, the university's lawyer accused him of electioneering, saying he was 'the David Duke of Arthur County running for office by attacking State U.'

    Two weeks after the column appeared, the district attorney filed a libel suit against The Tattler and its columnist.
    Based on your knowledge of the law, what must District Attorney Jones prove? How would he accomplish this? What is implied by the comment? What defenses are available to The Tattler and its columnist? What is the best defense? What arguments would they make? How do you think the judge and jury would rule in this case?

5. You are a picture editor at a wire service, and a free-lance photographer brings you some compelling pictures of hostages taken in the latest hot spot on the other side of the globe. You have dealt with this photographer before, but she has never brought you such dramatic pictures of guards pointing guns at handcuffed prisoners. The photographer offers you exclusive rights to the pictures, but says if you don't buy them she has others waiting to make offers. What questions do you ask the photographer about the photos? Do you buy them?

6. You are a copy editor at a newspaper, and a featured columnist has turned in a column about an outrageous new online computer site that shows movie clips of purported executions in various prisons. As you read the column, you wonder how real the clips are. The Web address is not included in the column. You think it should be included so that readers can evaluate the clips for themselves. You try a search on various words such as *execution* and *death row* but can't find the site. You try to call the columnist at home to get the Web address. She's not there. You are 30 minutes from deadline for shipping the page with the column on it. You have never had a problem with her columns before but now your suspicions are raised. Do you print it and hope the facts are right, or do you kill the column and hope readers don't complain about its absence?

7. Do enough research about a real ethical case to write up a case study. You can find real examples of ethical cases in such academic journals as the Journal of Mass Media Ethics or popular magazines such as American Journalism Review. Include all pertinent facts in the case, but draw no conclusions, and do not reveal how the actual case turned out. Share your case study with classmates, and discuss how each of you would have acted in the situation. Do not forget to consider the issues from all viewpoints; that means you have to determine who all the stakeholders are, including readers.

Beyond the Story

CHAPTER 12

Headlines: Precision, power and poetry

Writing headlines that are lively and informative, as well as accurate, is truly an art. And there is the additional challenge of making those lively, informative, accurate headlines fit into the allotted space. Headline writing is perhaps the most important skill in copy editing, and it is the one that takes the most effort to master.

Hurried readers often quickly skim the newspaper, perhaps reading only those stories whose compelling headlines demand a closer look. Headlines help the reader index the news of the day, to determine at a glance what the top stories are. They must entice readers, as well as summarize the stories in only a few well-chosen words.

You need to familiarize yourself with some terms used to denote headline styles and sizes:

A *down* style, widely used in today's newspapers, means capitalization of only the first word and any proper names in the headline. Papers such as The New York Times that use an *up* style capitalize every word in the headline, except articles, prepositions and conjunctions. Lowercase letters are easier to read, so you rarely see ALL-CAPS headlines.

Typeface refers to the look, or design, of the letters and numbers. Most publications adopt a "family" of typefaces — a group similar in appearance. Typefaces can be either *serif*, which have fine lines at the tops and bottoms of the letters— Times or Bookman, for example — or *sans serif*, without these flourishes — Futura or Helvetica, for example. Headlines can be written in either Roman (straight) or *Italics* (slanted) and *light* or **boldface** *weight*.

Page designers use a shorthand method to tell the copy editor the type of headline needed for a particular story. For example, a 2-36-2 order means you should write a two-column-wide, 36-point-high, two-line head. An "x" might be added to designate italics, or "B" for bold. Since there are 72 points per inch, two lines of 36-point type would be approximately 1 inch deep.

You also may be asked to write a variety of headline styles, sometimes more than one on a story. For example, you might be asked to write a *kicker* or *eyebrow*, wording in smaller type that reads into or expands on the main head below. A *hammer* is a reversed kicker, possibly only a word or two, in larger (and perhaps bolder) type than the lines below it. Or the designer might call for a main head with a *drop head*, or *readout*. These lines in smaller type, which may be italicized and/or lighter than the main head, either summarize the story or present an angle secondary to the main head.

Because headline-writing is such an important skill, which is honed with experience, talented headline writers are highly valued by their copy desks. The exercises in this chapter are designed to help you recognize good headlines as well as spot problems. They will give you practice in the fundamentals of headline writing.

Exercises

1. Find a headline in your local newspaper that you think is inaccurate, is poorly phrased or otherwise needs improvement. Try rewriting it within the same count, or approximately the same number of characters.

2. Find a headline in your local newspaper, or perhaps a magazine, that you think is particularly well written. What do you like about it?

3. Each of the following headlines has a problem. Revise each, keeping the headline about the same number of characters per line.

> Chinese ban
> balloonists from
> their airspace

> Ford, Carter
> want censor
> for president

> Water main break affects service

> Rehnquist may find
> himself more in the
> limelight than ever

> Commissioner says
> decision on tax will
> be appealed in court

> Area girls' teams are
> lacking in experience

If your searching for
a home, here's advice

Exhibit of Frank Lloyd
Wright designs opens

4. Write a headline for each of the stories in Chapter 6, according to specifications given by your instructor.

5. Write a one-column, 18-point, three-line headline for the following story:

FORT-DE-FRANCE, Martinique (AP) — A Club Med where striking workers detained 373 tourists will shut down until a labor dispute is resolved, the Paris-based resort chain said yesterday.

Police in riot gear raided the resort on the Caribbean island of Martinique Sunday night to free the guests.

Unions claimed four employees were injured during the raid, and some were treated for inhalation of tear gas. The guests — most of them French, German and Italian — were not hurt.

About 200 employees of the Club Med along the south coast struck last Wednesday to demand 8 percent raises. When negotiations broke down Saturday, the workers blocked the hotel entrances and refused to let guests leave.

Tourists said they were not mistreated. The resort's pools and other facilities remained open, and managers took over cooking.

After the raid, police buses took guests to other hotels. The resort will remain closed until there is a labor agreement, said Club Med spokesman Christian Mure.

-30-

6. Write headlines for the following stories according to specifications from your instructor.

   a. Wildfire

   FILLMORE, Calif. (AP) — Officials here in Southern California turned their attention to the threat of floods Saturday after firefighters contained a wildfire that encompassed over 12,000 acres in Ventura County.

   The fire, which began one week ago, stripped the rolling hills surrounding Pole Creek of brush, and runoff from winter rains could swell the creek and threaten Fillmore, a farming town of 13,000 residents 45 miles west-northwest of Los Angeles.

   "A number of drainages will be impacted during a heavy season of rain," said Capt. Mike Lindbery of the county fire department. "We have a team of 160 experts in there looking to see if seeding and planting is needed and where it needs to go. They will make assessments to mitigate a potential flooding problem."

   Flooding from the creek caused $700,000 damage in 1995.

   "There is a disaster on the horizon if we don't do something," said Chief Pat Askren of the Fillmore Fire Department. "We're trying to do what we need to protect the city."

   Bert Rapp, a city engineer, is to submit a report to the City Council listing the steps that should be taken against flooding, including sandbag brigades and installation of concrete railings to divert floodwaters.

   "It could rain at any time," Rapp said. "The projection this year is that we would have early, heavy rains. So we don't have a lot of time." ...

   -30-

   b. Boats

   SACRAMENTO, Calif., Oct. 24 (AP) – Air-quality regulators in California have proposed rules that are tougher than Federal pollution standards to limit emissions from personal watercraft and motorboats.

The rules proposed by the state's Air Resources Board would force manufacturers to make cleaner engines for personal watercraft, like Jet Skis, and motorboats.

Bill Rush, a spokesman for Californians United to Save Boating, which represents recreational boat owners, criticized the proposed regulations, saying they would make boat engines too expensive and hurt the state's $11 billion boating and related industries. About 500,000 motorboats with outboard engines and personal watercraft ply the state's lakes and rivers.

"We think these recommendations are really a good example of over-regulation that's going to threaten boating and boating-related businesses in California," Mr. Rush said.

The Federal Environmental Protection Agency adopted standards for the first time in 1996 to cut emission levels from the engines of recreational boats, setting a goal of a 75 percent reduction by 2006. Those rules went into effect this year.

The board found that the Federal standards were too lax to reduce smog and proposed its own standards, which would cut emissions 65 percent more than what the E.P.A. standards call for by 2008. A public hearing is scheduled for Dec. 10.

The two-cycle engines that power Jet Skis are highly inefficient, producing noise and smoke and even spewing raw fuel from the tailpipe. In seven hours, a Jet Ski produces as much pollution as a 1998 car driven for 100,000 miles, the board said.

The regulations cover two-cycle engines and more expensive and efficient four-cycle engines that mainly power motorboats. On a weekend summer day, both types of engines pump 750 tons of hydrocarbons and nitrogen oxides into the air over California's lakes and rivers.

The board said it thought regulations would not hurt engine sales in California, which accounts for a 10th of all outboard motor sales in the United States.

It estimated that engine prices would rise an average of 14 percent — $150 to $2,300 – but that the higher cost of more efficient engines would be partly offset by savings in fuel and maintenance.

Mr. Rush said the real cost was likely to be many times larger and would take a huge toll on California's boating industry, the second largest in the nation, behind Michigan's. There are 3.5 million recreational boat owners in California.

The board's proposal came amid complaints from environmentalists and water quality agencies about the possible carcinogen MTBE, a component of gasoline left in lakes by personal watercraft. Earlier this month, a Federal judge upheld an ordinance banning two-cycle engines from Lake Tahoe.

California, with the worst air pollution in the nation, has the unique power among the states to set its own emission standards. The board's standards are typically stricter than their Federal counterparts.

-30-

c. Cancer studies

BY KEVIN HOFFMAN
THE ASSOCIATED PRESS

Women can reduce their risk of colon cancer by eating lots of fruits and vegetables rich in the B-vitamin folate, a study found.

And in a second study, doctors from the University of Vermont provided encouraging evidence that a new procedure may allow surgeons to reduce dramatically the number of lymph nodes they remove during breast-cancer surgery, sparing women some of the pain and possible complications.

The colon-cancer study, in today's issue of the Annals of Internal Medicine, tracked 121,700 U.S. nurses from 1976 to 1994. It found that women who had a high intake of folate from food or from multivitamins for at least 15 years were 75 percent less likely to get colon cancer.

A folate-rich diet was defined as one consisting of at least four to five servings a day of leafy, green vegetables and fruits.

Foods rich in folate includ spinach, romaine lettuce and broccoli. Orange juice is another good source, as are fortified breakfast cereals.

"We don't want people to think that their diet doesn't matter, that they don't need to exercise, that they can just take a pill and prevent cancer," said Dr. Edward Giovannucci of Harvard Medical School. "But someone taking a folate in the long term will have a 75 percent reduced risk."

While the study focused on women, increased levels of folic acid could help men, too, researchers said.

Dr. Kim Jessup, director of gastrointestinal oncology at the University of Pittsburgh Cancer Institute, questioned why it takes 15 years of eating folate for women to reduce their risk for cancer.

"This makes you think it might be a relatively weak effect," said Jessup, noting studies that have shown aspirin can prevent 50 percent of colon cancers when used for more than one year.

The American Cancer Society estimates that 95,600 people will be diagnosed with colon cancer this year, and 47,700 will die of the disease.

The breast-cancer study reported that just as doctors have learned that they can often safely remove just the lump rather than the whole cancerous breast, they are now experimenting with the idea that not all the lymph nodes need to come out, either.

Doctors from the University of Vermont cited a new procedure that involves injecting radioactive material around the tumor and then removing only the nodes that eventually absorb it.

"It's quick and easy to precisely locate the node before ever making an incision. That's the key advantage," said Dr. David Krag, who helped pioneer the technique.

Krag trained 11 other surgeons to use the method. They reported the results of testing on 443 patients.

They found that if the gamma ray counter picked up a signal, the procedure was 97 percent accurate at pinpointing all the cancerous nodes. However, the procedure missed cancerous nodes in 13 of the 114 women with spreading cancer.

In an accompanying analysis, Dr. V. Suzanne Klimberg of the University of Arkansas and others said the chance of missing cancerous nodes was the main drawback.

Krag said that by doubling the dose of radioactive material, it may be possible to lower the number of missed cases substantially.

Doctors will test this idea in a large study sponsored by the National Cancer Institute, that will begin in about three months. The sentinel node procedure will be tested against standard lymph-node removal in about 4,000 women.

The primary advantage of the new approach is that it removes about 50 times less tissue than standard surgery. Krag said doctors take out one to three grams of tissue instead of the usual 100 to 150 grams.

-30-

d. Snake

BY KAREN LEE ZINER
KNIGHT RIDDER NEWSPAPERS

PUTNAM, Conn. — Earlier this week, Christopher Paquin found himself a bit too tightly wrapped; caught in the potentially fatal embrace of his 19-foot, 260-pound Burmese python, "Squeeze," who tried to eat him.

Things went awry when the agitated snake uprooted the toilet in the bathroom where Paquin left the animal while he cleaned his cage.

As water gushed and the snake "tried to take the toilet with her," Paquin seized the snake. "But I grabbed her too far down," he said.

As man battled beast in a knotty-pine sunroom, the reptile pinned Paquin, who weighs 200 pounds, to the floor. Twining around him like the coils of Medusa, the reptile constricted, yawned widely with its loosely hinged jaws and clamped "down to the bone."

"I went down on my knees right here. This is all my blood," Paquin, 27, said, pointing to a stained carpet at 10 Marshall St.

As his friend Tammy Breton watched in shock, Paquin hollered at her to get the snake off him. Breton tried, with pliers, but Paquin yelled that it was hurting the snake. Breton then dialed 911.

"She was in a panic," according to Police Sgt. Robert Riley. "She said a very large snake was eating her boyfriend on the arm, and wrapping itself all around his body and chest."

When the three officers arrived, they found "quite a sight ... this guy was being devoured all the way close to the shoulder," said Riley.

"It hurt like a vise. When the teeth were going into my bone, I could feel it," said Paquin. "When somebody asked, 'How did it hurt?' I said, 'Let me cut off your leg.'

"I don't know how they got it off me," said Paquin, but by pulling and tugging, the three officers eventually separated Paquin from his snake.

They prodded it into another room, and slammed the door.

Paquin, rushed by ambulance to a nearby hospital, sustained 35 punctures and slash wounds, from thumb to forearm. After his arm was X-rayed for stray serpent's teeth, and then cleaned and immobilized in a cast, he went home.

Meanwhile, he gave the go-ahead for his snake to be put to death.

First stunning it with carbon dioxide from a fire extinguisher, then further subduing it with electrical prods, police, firefighters and Department of Environmental Protection officers "dispatched it" with three .22-caliber shots to the head.

"Then," said Riley, "they beheaded.

"They tried two things. One was like a hunting knife," said a neighbor who declined to give her name. "The other looked like a cleaver. I think they had to saw it a little bit.

"It squirmed around in the backyard for a few hours," she said, "even after the head was cut off."

Across the country, as the pet trade in Burmese pythons flourishes and sizable numbers are exported annually from Southeast Asia to meet the demand for the popular brown-and-yellow tropical constrictor, similar stories appear in the headlines.

Two years ago exactly, New York papers reported the death of a Bronx man who was found in a pool of blood with his 13-foot Burmese python coiled around his torso, and a live chicken — apparently the intended meal — in a box a few feet away.

Earlier that year, San Diego paramedics beheaded a family's nine-foot pet python with a hacksaw after it wrapped itself around a pregnant woman's stomach and bit her buttocks, then coiled around the woman's husband.

This summer, a relatively small Burmese python turned up in a box of tomatoes in a Chicago fast-food restaurant.

-30-

e. Fatal

BY DEMORRIS LEE
RALEIGH NEWS AND OBSERVER STAFF WRITER

ARCHER LODGE — Authorities released the names of three of the four people killed in a head-on accident on a rural highway in eastern Johnston County on Monday night.

Tommy Ray Tinsley, 43, of Selma, Sandra Williams Jackson, 43, of Four Oaks; and Bryan Keith Johnson, 28, of Clayton, were pronounced dead at the scene or while en route to a hospital. The fourth victim has yet to be identified.

Highway Patrol Sgt. C.S. Taylor said that Tinsley was speeding and under the influence of alcohol when the red Pontiac Grand Prix he was driving crossed the center line on N.C. 42 and struck a blue Mercury driven by Johnson.

The investigation also determined that Tinsely was traveling 75 mph to 80 mph in a 55 mph zone, Taylor said.

"We were able to determine that Tinsley was under the influence once we got him to the hospital," Taylor said. "There was no alcohol connected to the driver of the Mercury or no indication that he was speeding."

The accident occurred about 7 p.m. on N.C. 42, a mile east of the N.C. 39 intersection and about 12 miles east of Clayton.

Tinsley, Johnson and the unidentified front-seat passenger of the Pontiac died at the scene. Jackson, who was riding in the back seat of the Pontiac, died while being airlifted to Duke Hospital.

Johnson was returning to his home from Wilson, where he worked at Best Brand, a distributing company, when the accident happened, said his aunt Joyce Sanders. He was a truck driver for the company.

"He was a family man who loved people," Sanders said. "He loved doing for other people and he never met a stranger. He was just wonderful and way too young to have his life taken away from him."

The father of two loved to spend time with his family. Sanders said that Johnson's wife, Chandra, and his two kids, Bryan Jr., 3, and daughter Robbie, 2, meant the world to him.

"He loved his children, and he was a real family man," she said. "We are not going to let them forget him. We are going to make sure that his kids know what kind of person he was."

Sanders, who said Johnson was more like a brother to her, added that this ordeal has been a nightmare.

"It is a tragedy and this is something I wouldn't want anyone to go through," she said. "It's like a bad dream.

"When we lost his mother four years ago, we helped each other through it. He was more than just my nephew, he was a friend. I will make sure that his kids remember his friendly spirit."

There will be a visitation for Johnson at Mount Vernon United Church of Christ in Clayton from 6 to 8 p.m. Friday. The funeral service will be at 2 p.m. Saturday at the church.

Funeral services for Jackson will be at 2 p.m. Thursday at Juniper Grove Disciple Church in Four Oaks.

Arrangements for Tinsley were not complete at press time.

-30-

CHAPTER 13

An eye for news: Editing photos

Photography is such an important part of journalism that a word was coined to bring the two concepts even closer together: *photojournalism*. And photojournalism emerged only relatively recently, although it took from 1839, when photography was born, until the early 20th century before journalists began exploiting the medium. Of course, photographic reproductions appeared in newspapers in the 19th century, but they were used more for illustrations than news. Today, we think of photos in newspapers primarily for their news or informational value (although photo illustrations often appear in feature sections).

Until recently, most news photos focused tightly on a single event or person and left out as much extraneous material as possible. One reason to avoid loose framing is the historically poor reproduction quality of newspapers. That is changing; newspaper reproduction of photos has improved with higher-quality, offset printing and the introduction of color. Another reason for promoting tightly cropped photos is that they do not need to run very large to be readable, leaving more room for other elements on the page. Modern photographers have more flexibility. Copy editors must now recognize that thoughtless cropping of photos may be as harmful as cutting long feature stories from the bottom. Editing stories and photos requires equal care.

At some newspapers, picture editing is left to the photo desk; at others, the copy editors and page designers make editing decisions. In either case, each picture that appears in the newspaper should be carefully selected using the same criteria for news value as would be used for a story. In general, photos should be cropped to eliminate irrelevant information, but this usually is done by the photographer. Finally, the picture should run at the appropriate scale; that is, it should be large enough to see important details and to have an impact. One "rule of thumb" is to run pictures with subjects large enough, at minimum, so that the smallest significant face is at least as large as your thumbnail.

Cropping photos involves both the reshaping of the photo, that is, changing the proportions and determining the size of the picture when it is printed. Sizing of photos can be done with a proportion wheel, mathematically or electronically. More and more graphics are scanned and edited electronically. Today's editors should become familiar with the fundamentals of the various photo editing programs even if they leave the details to the photo staff. These programs are very powerful and allow for many effects to be used. Editors should be extremely cautious about doing anything that might undermine the integrity of the photo.

All photos should be accompanied by a cutline or caption and a credit line. When pictures do not accompany a story — stand-alone or "wild" photos — they will usually have a headline or lead-in, also often called a catchline. Newspapers vary on the placement and style of the catchline.

Writing good cutlines is as much an art as writing good headlines. As anyone who reads National Geographic knows, people will read cutlines even if they don't read a word of the story. Cutlines should name all identifiable people in the photo, usually from left to right, using a directional indicator such as "from left" if more than two people are pictured or simply "left" or "right" if only two are pictured. (There is no need to use a directional if a man and woman are pictured and their names are gender-specific.) The cutline should avoid such descriptive clichés as "looks on" or anything else that states the obvious. Also, cutlines are usually written in the present tense, which sometimes becomes awkward when the time element must be included in the cutline. In such cases, a second sentence in which the past tense and the time element are used may be necessary. Other rules for cutlines include not interpreting what the subject feels — it should be obvious from the picture — and telling, when warranted, of any special circumstances surrounding the photo, such as special techniques or equipment used by the photographer. Finally, it should go without saying that all information should be accurate, yet all too often names in cutlines, when compared to those in stories, don't match.

Exercises

1. Look through a number of editions of the same newspaper and determine its cutline style. Do you notice violations of the style? Keep looking at cutlines, because if you look at enough you will find one in which the name of a person is different in the accompanying story. Can you find such a discrepancy?

2. How would you crop this photo? After you have cropped it, how high will it be if it runs 51 picas, 8 points (four columns wide)? Write a cutline with catchline and credit from the following information (note any missing or additional information you would need): Penn State midfielder Sonje Volla (12) and goalie Jamie Smith (1) stop a scoring attempt by a Northwestern player during Friday's match. The Lions Beat the Wildcats 4-1. (Photo by Lisa Beard — Daily News.)

3. Size this photo for a 38-pica (3-column) space. How deep will it run? For the photo below, write a cutline with catchline and credit from the following information for the photo below (note any additional information you would need): John Cocolin enjoys a nice spring day while selling hot dogs Thursday on the corner of Allen St. and College Ave. He is retired but spends four hours a day at his stand. (Photo by Kirsten Gurka — Daily News.)

4. Crop the photo below and then size it for a 38-pica (3-column) space. Mark the horizontal and vertical crops. How many picas deep will your reproduction be? Write a cutline, catchline and credit from the following information (note any additional information you would need): Carrie Spencer of State College cools off at a fountain on South Allen Street during the Arts Festival Friday. The festival runs through Sunday. The high temperature Friday was 84 degrees. (Photo by Dan Murphy — Daily News.)

5. Crop and size this photo for a 51-pica, 8-point (4-column) space. How deep will it be? Write a cutline, catchline and credit line from the following information (note any additional information you need): Penn State running back Curtis Enis (39) scored one of his three touchdowns against the University of Southern California in the Kickoff Classic Saturday at the Meadowlands in New Jersey. Penn State won 24-7. No. 4 is USC linebacker Mark Cusano. (Photo by Steve Manuel — Daily News.)

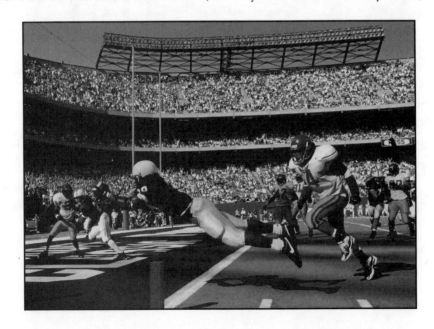

6. Assume this photo will run full frame in a 51-pica, 8-point (4-column) space. What will the depth of the reproduction be in picas and points? With cropping, what is the minimum acceptable depth of the photo in picas and points? Write a cutline, catchline and credit line based on the following information supplied by the photographer (note any additional information needed): A municipal waste truck owned by Fred Carson Sanitary Disposal Service gets stuck on a broken small bridge it was crossing Friday along Route 26 outside State College. The bridge provides access to two homes. (Photo by Craig Houtz — Centre Daily Times.)

7. The following four pictures were all shot at the same event. Use some or all of this information for cutlines in the following exercises: Jim Redyke owner of Dykon of Tulsa, Oklahoma, connects the ignition wires to a blasting machine before the demolition of the West Penn/Allegheny Power Co. plant in Milesburg, Pa., Thursday. The plant was demolished in two stages. First the concrete stack, which was 270 feet tall, was brought down. Then explosives in the 60-foot steel and aluminum structure adjacent to the stack were ignited. The demolition caused a huge dust cloud. Dykon used 70 pounds of explosives to bring both structures down while 80 spectators looked on. (Photos by Michele Mott — Centre Daily Times.)

   a. Pick the best picture for the front page, size and crop it as you think appropriate, then write a cutline and credit line to go with a story (that will jump off the front page).

   b. Using the same set of pictures, pick two for a combination photo and story package. Crop, size and arrange the two photos for a 64-pica, 10-point (five-column) space with headline and story. Write a single cutline and credit line for both photos.

c. Pick three of the photos below for a five-column space of any depth you choose. Crop, size and arrange the photos for the space, leaving room for a story and headline. How deep will each of the photos be in your arrangement? Write a single cutline or several cutlines as you deem appropriate.

8. Crop and size this photo for a 25-pica (two-column) space. How deep will it be? How deep would it be in a 38-pica (three-column) space? Write a cutline, catchline and credit based on the following information supplied by the Associated Press: A0320 03/09/99 16:48 J AP PS AP A DC WX104 WEA WINTER STORM A Washington policeman makes his way past the White House on his mountain bike as heavy winter snowfall paralyzed the nation's capitol and the surrounding metropolitan area Tuesday, March 9. The snow caused several hundred traffic accidents across Virginia and prompted school districts to cancel early. (AP PHOTO/KAMENKO PAJIC)

9. Crop and size this photo for a 38-pica (three-column) space. How deep will it be in picas and points? Write a cutline, catchline and credit based on the following information supplied by the Associated Press: A1939 03/10/99 08:17 J AP PS AP I IND DEL103 INDIA TIBET Chinese President Jiang Zemin is burned in effigy during a rally marking the 40th anniversary of the Chinese occupation of Tibet Wednesday March 10. More than 5,000 protesters marched through downtown New Dehli to the parliament house and then burned 40 Chinese flags. (AP Photo/John McConnico)

CHAPTER 14

Showing the story: Editing information graphics

Newspaper graphics have undergone a revolution in the last 20 years. There is probably no better example of the coming of age of graphics than the weather map in USA Today. Soon after USA Today and its expanded weather coverage appeared, newspapers across the country copied the innovative map and beefed up their graphics departments to match. Those that were capable of printing their maps in color did so. Suddenly, newspapers everywhere recognized the informational value of graphics of all kinds, including tables, graphs, diagrams and maps. Not that they hadn't been used before, but now they were given new prominence.

Copy editors play an important role in both the production of newspaper graphics and their use. When a story about a plane crash, for example, is going to run, editors know readers want to know where the crash occurred, so they will order a map from the graphics department or hope one of the wire services will supply one. But just as likely, and more so in the future, copy editors themselves may go into the newspaper's database to obtain and modify an existing map, inserting a pointer box with a label showing where the crash occurred. Indeed, for the simplest charts, tables and other graphics, it is increasingly likely that the copy editor will be called upon to provide the graphic, leaving the art department to work on more complex illustrations and graphics. Copy editors who can prepare graphics as well as edit stories and write headlines are very much in demand. And the proliferation of computers and software in the newsroom can make even minimally artistic editors look like graphic gurus.

Graphics are used for a number of reasons. One is to break up type. Editors know that many readers are turned off by unrelieved columns of type. Graphics help to break up the grayness. They also provide multiple ways to entice readers into a story. Graphics that accompany a story are probably better read than the story itself. The most important reason to use graphics is to make understanding information easier for the reader. For example, when the president sends his annual budget to Congress, editors often use pie charts to illustrate where most of the projected spending will go. Charts both inform the reader and illustrate a story that may not otherwise have a strong visual component.

In addition to maps and pie charts, other types of graphics are the line, or fever, chart; bar, or column, chart; table (text displayed in columns and rows); diagram; and logo. All but the simplest graphics should have a few elements in common. They should have a title, a source line and a credit line. Inside the graphic is a blurb, or copy block, that explains what the graphic depicts.

Copy editors are the last line of defense for assuring the accuracy of graphics that appear in the paper. No matter how fancy they are or how necessary it seems to break up type, if the graphic isn't informative and accurate, it is hurting rather than helping the newspaper. Copy editors must make sure that the graphic is accurate, but they also need to make sure that the information contained in the graphic matches the facts in the story — to the extent they overlap. Of course, a well-designed graphic and a well-edited story will not often need to have repetitive information. In checking a graphic, you must make sure that numbers add up. Pie charts should always add up to 100 percent. Place names must be spelled accurately, and geographic locations must be in their correct relative positions. Readers spend time looking at graphics and will spot any errors that aren't caught. If, for example, a business story says sales increased from $125 million to $140 million and the graphic shows a 15 percent increase, the copy editor must have the art department correct the discrepancy. In addition to accuracy, the copy desk can assure that graphics adhere to the newspaper's graphics style, just as stories must follow a style. And the last check the copy editor should make is the same as the first question that should be asked when assigning a graphic: Is it appropriate? A map of the United States that indicates a plane crash in New York state is hardly helpful for the average North American newspaper reader.

Exercises

1. From various newspapers and magazines, collect examples of the different types of graphics: line or fever chart, bar chart, pie chart, table, map, diagram and logo. Discuss what information is best illustrated by each graphic form.

2. Check newspapers and magazines for stories that could have used a graphic. What type of graphic would have been best to use?

3. Use the following stock market information to sketch out various charts. Try different ways of charting the information to emphasize or de-emphasize time and the degree of change. For example, change the scale on the left side so that each gradation of change is a doubling from the previous one, or change the time scale across the bottom to focus only on most recent milestones.

Dow Jones Industrial Average Milestones

May 3, 1999: Breaks 11,000 closing at 11,014.69.

Mar. 28, 1999: Breaks 10,000 closing at 10,006.78.

Apr. 6, 1998: Breaks 9,000 closing at 9,033.23.

July 16 1997: Breaks 8,000, closing at 8,038.88.

Feb. 13, 1997: Breaks 7,000, closing at 7,022.44.

Oct. 14, 1996: Breaks 6,000, closing at 6,010.00.

Nov. 21, 1995: Breaks 5,000, closing at 5,023.55.

Feb. 23, 1995: Breaks 4,000, closing at 4,003.33.

Apr. 17, 1991: Breaks 3,000, closing at 3,004.46.

Jan. 8, 1987: Breaks 2,000, closing at 2,002.25.

Nov. 14, 1972: Breaks 1,000, closing at 1,003.16.

Jan. 12, 1906: Breaks 100, closing at 100.25.

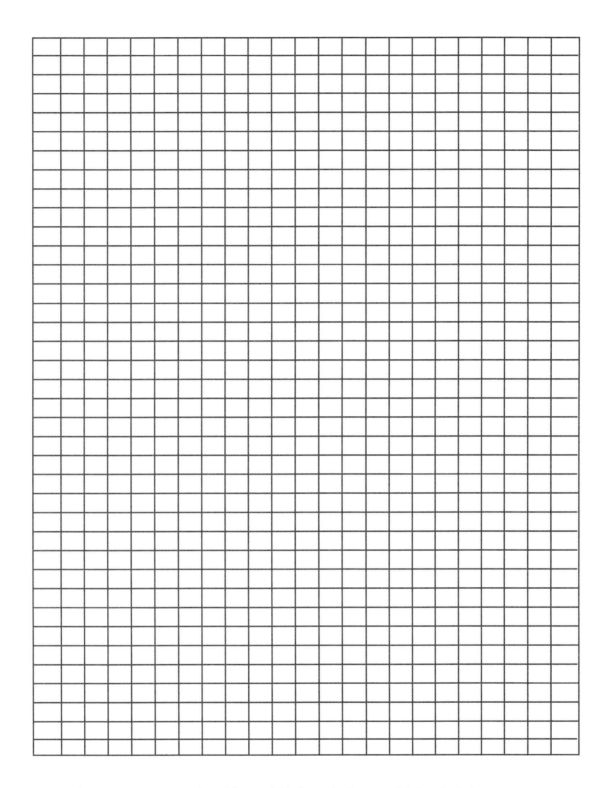

4. Use the Consumer Price Index tables available from the Bureau of Labor Statistics (http://stats.bls.gov/cpihome.htm) to gather information and sketch a chart comparing the stock market's performance as measured by the Dow Jones industrial average in the previous exercise with inflation. For example, $1,000 invested in the Dow on Nov. 14, 1972, would have been worth $9,000 on April 6, 1998. What would $1,000 worth of goods in 1972 cost in 1998 according to the CPI? Create a graphic showing this relationship.

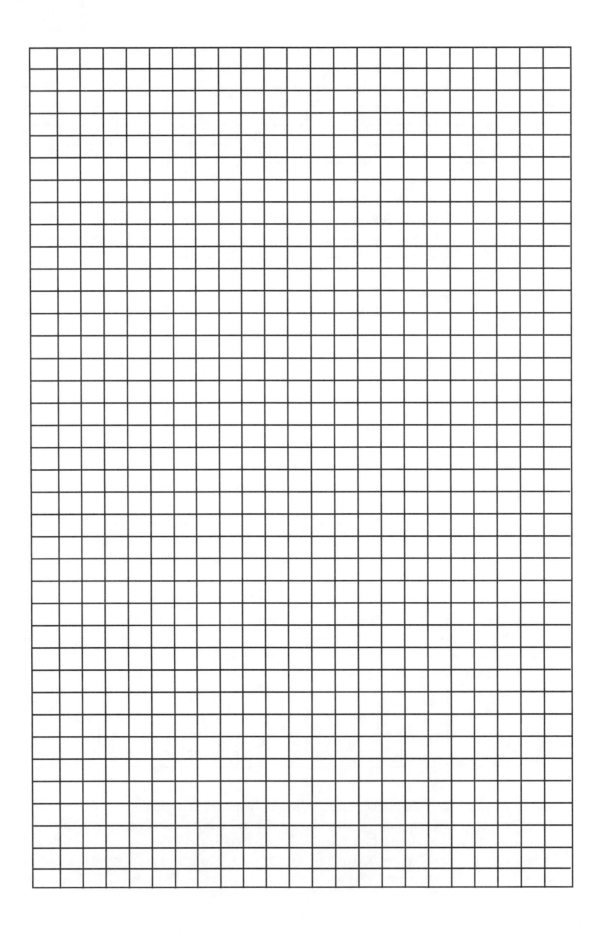

5. Sketch a series of charts using the following information as reported by the U.S. Department of Agriculture. Try combining the different data in one chart to emphasize various trends.

Year	Number of Farms
1940	6.2 million
1950	5.8 million
1960	3.9 million
1970	3.0 million
1980	2.5 million
1990	2.0 million

Year	Average Farm Size
1940	174 acres
1950	213 acres
1960	297 acres
1970	374 acres
1980	426 acres
1990	469 acres

Year	People in Farm Occupations
1940	8.99 million
1950	6.85 million
1960	4.13 million
1970	2.88 million
1980	2.81 million
1990	2.86 million

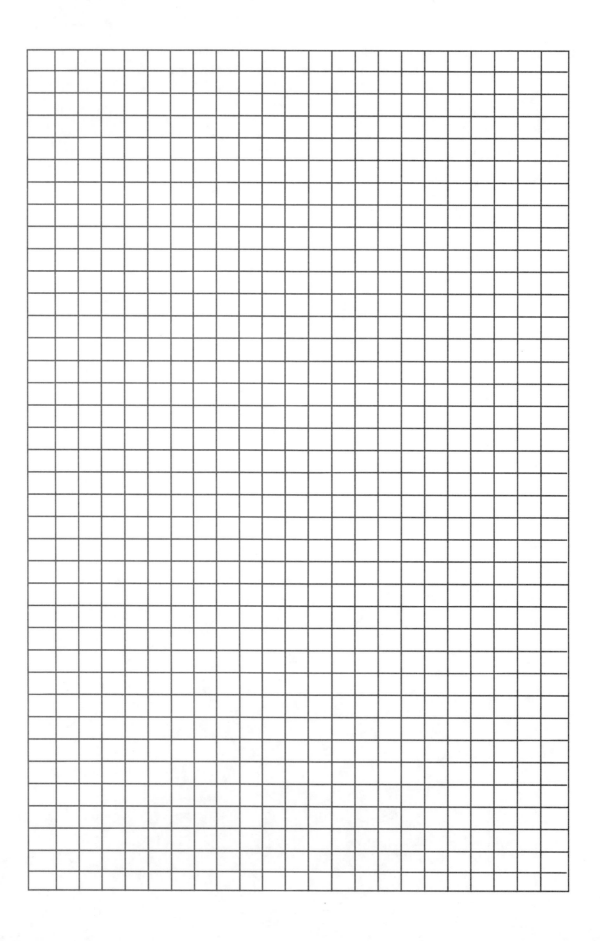

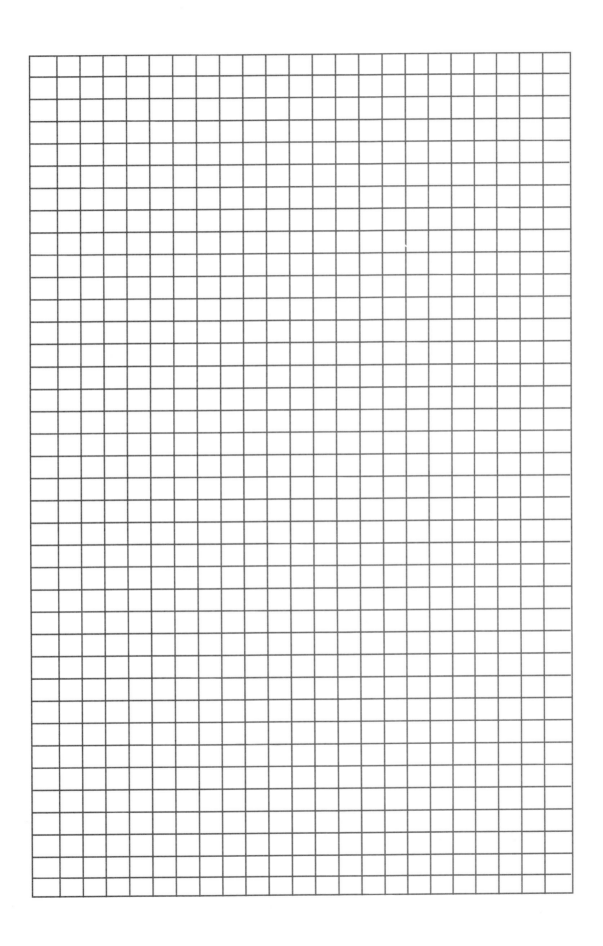

6. Configure a graphic using the following figures and information to go with a story about Pepsi's introduction of Storm into the market. Storm is a lemon-lime flavored soda intended to compete with Sprite and 7-Up.

Soda (12 oz.)	Caffeine (mg)
Barq's Root Beer	23.0
Canada Dry	30.0
Coca-Cola/Diet Coke	45.6
Diet Canada Dry	1.2
Diet Pepsi	37.0
Diet Rite Cola	0.0
Dr Pepper	39.6
Jolt	71.2
Kick Citrus	54.0
Mellow Yellow	52.8
Minute Maid Orange	0.0
Mountain Dew/Diet	55.0
Mr. Pibb	40.8
Mug Root Beer	0.0
Pepsi-Cola	37.2
Pepsi One	55.5
RC Cola/Diet	36.0
7-Up	0.0
Shasta Cola/Diet/Cherry Cola	44.4
Sprite	0.0
Storm	38.0
Sugar-free Mr. Pibb	58.8
Sunkist Orange	40.0
Surge	51.0
Tab	46.8

Sources: U.S. Food and Drug Administration, National Soft Drink Association, Bunker and McWilliams, Pepsi

7. Create a graphic to illustrate the following information from Catalyst regarding the 2.9 million women in managerial or administrative jobs in the private sector:

Group	Percentage
White	89.7
African-American	6.6
Hispanic	5.2
Asian and other groups	2.5

8. Create a graphic to illustrate corporate distribution of supermarket sales of breakfast cereals (in billions of dollars for year ending August 1998). Total annual sales are $7.14 billion.

Kellogg	$2.3
General Mills	$2.2
Post General Foods	$1.2
Quaker Oats	$0.61
Store brands	$0.55
Malt-O-Meal	$0.18
Generic	$0.10

   Source: Information Resources Inc.

9. Create a time line that charts President Clinton's job performance as measured by one of the major polls. You will need to find the performance figures at www.ropercenter.uconn.edu/presapp/charts.htm. Include in the chart major events that occurred during Clinton's presidency. You can find these by looking in an almanac or in year-end newspaper stories for each year of his presidency.

10. Using the presidential job performance data from the site in the previous exercise, graph President Clinton's job performance ratings against President Reagan's ratings, since both men served second terms. See whether any interesting trends appear when you add economic performance figures to these graphics. The economic data may come from a number of sources; one is the monthly consumer confidence survey conducted by the Conference Board. This data can be gathered by doing searches in an online database on the key words *consumer confidence*.

The balancing act: Designing pages

Design in newspapers is important because good-looking pages are reader friendly and allow the reader to move from graphic to story with ease. Well-designed pages attract readers and keep them reading longer. In addition, design is an immediate indicator of the personality of the newspaper. Compare, for example, the pinstriped, buttoned-down design of The Wall Street Journal and the studied casualness of USA Today. But perhaps most important, good design helps the reader immediately grasp the editors' ratings of the importance of various stories on a page. Above all, good design should serve news judgment, not the other way around.

Over the years, page design has tended to get simpler, eschewing the garish makeup and screaming headlines of turn-of-the-century newspapers — and even some more recent ones. Today, with few exceptions, layout and design are modular, which means that each story or story-art combination can be enclosed by a quadrangle. Design is a way of telling readers that some thought has gone into the packaging of stories. Contrast this with the older layout styles that were either uniformly dull or used a hodgepodge makeup style that gave the reader no help in following a story around the page.

Although the design of newspapers has always been the prerogative of the editorial staff, only with the advent of computers has the ability to directly translate that design into camera-ready pages moved from the shop into the newsroom. Computerized pagination has brought design and execution so close together that it is now difficult to tell where one leaves off and the other begins. Despite the introduction of computers and software programs such as Adobe PageMaker or Quark XPress into the production process, it is still useful for beginners (and even seasoned pros) to sketch out a page design on paper before using a pagination program to execute the page. Paper sketches can save time and aggravation. Particularly when one is learning layout, it is useful to separate the issue of learning to design pages from the process of learning to use complex computer programs.

Good design begins with an understanding of various principles such as balance, contrast, proportion, symmetry and rhythm. It extends to the smallest details. The principles and practices are used in conjunction with editors' news judgments to give a page purpose and to anticipate readers' interests.

Exercises

1. Buy copies of a half-dozen newspapers on the same day, avoiding Sundays or major news days. Make notes on what you see as similarities and differences in design at various levels. For example, analyze the three main elements of newspaper design: headlines, pictures and body text. But also look at details such as caption treatments, bylines and credit lines.

2. Assume a broadsheet newspaper page with a six-column format is 78 picas wide by 21 1/2 inches deep. The gutters between columns are 1 pica wide. How wide will each column be in picas and points? (Remember that there are 12 points per pica.) If a photo is three columns wide, how many picas is that?

Regarding column measures: If type is set in an "odd" or "bastard" measure so that two columns of type cover three standard columns, how wide will each bastard-measure column be? What if the type is set three columns on four? What if the type is set two on three inside a box that uses a 1-pica gutter between the type and the box? (*Note:* You may wish to enlarge the layout grids found at the end of the chapter for additional practice.)

3. Take several pages from one of the newspapers you bought for the first exercise and copy the pages onto dummies based on measurements you take from those pages. Start with uncomplicated inside pages and work up to open pages or section fronts. Specify where headlines go and how big they should be, using the appropriate headline specification form. You will need to include space for any graphics or pictures and accompanying cutlines. Finally, you must show the flow of the type, including jumps, if any. Remember to give the slug, or working name, for each story, photo or graphic. Be sure to indicate headline specifications in standard columns/point size/number of lines form. Do the same for any drop heads.

4. Look at story, headline and photo combinations in various newspapers and sketch out different ways a story, headline and photo can be packaged while remaining modular. You should be able to come up with at least six ways. Often, one package can be a mirror image of another. Consider which combinations work best.

5. Take the stories listed in the following news budget and dummy them in a two-column space that runs on the left side the full length of a six-column broadsheet page, 78 picas wide by 21 1/2 inches deep. Be sure to indicate headline sizes. Stories can be trimmed as much as 10 percent without getting approval from the originating desk. Stories are listed in order of importance.

School board — 15 inches

Hospital donations — 10 inches

Summer fest — 10 inches

Blood drive — 5 inches

6. Use the following stories from a news budget to dummy an open section front for local news. The page is a six-column broadsheet page, 78 picas wide by 21 1/2 inches deep. You need to leave space across the top for the section flag; it is 2 inches deep. Stories can be trimmed up to 10 percent without getting approval from the originating desk. The policy is not to jump stories. Major photos must run; if a mug shot is available you can use your discretion on what size to run it or whether to run it on the main page or not at all. Except for the lead story, stories are not listed in order of importance.

Lead story, City Council discusses new municipal building — 14 inches, mug shot available

Circus opens five-day run — 12 inches with 3-column-by-10-inch photo

Bank robbery, suspects at large — 13 inches

School bus accident, no injuries — 12 inches

Locally owned business expanding — 12 inches, mug shot available

Highway interchange planned near mall — 7 inches

7. Take a front page from a newspaper you used in one of the previous exercises, and use a marker to draw boxes around all elements that are not photos, headlines or text related to stories that at least begin on that page. Determine how much of the page is devoted to teasers or refers to stories inside the newspaper.

8. Design a six-column, standard-size front page that uses all or some of the following stories, photos and graphics. Stories can jump. Photos and graphics must run as specified, except mug shots, which you may use. If you use them, they must run either one column by 2 inches or a half column by 1 inch. The newspaper's nameplate is 2 inches deep, and it runs the full-page width under a row of three 1-inch-deep teaser boxes.

   Lead story, governor charged with fraud — 20 inches, two-column by 4-inch photo available. Refer box to four inside sidebar stories needed.

   Sidebar to lead story, profile of prosecutor who pursued governor — 15 inches, mug shot available.

   4,000 run in city marathon in record cold — 13 inches, five-column by 4.5-inch photo, refer to two sidebars.

   City Council expected to approve Skyway project after year of debate — 12 inches.

   Jobless rate increases after six months of decline — 10 inches, with a one-column by 3-inch graphic.

   Congress debates Social Security overhaul — 12 inches, multiple mug shots available.

9. Gather four or five pages from newspapers or magazines in which the display type is in color. Why do you think the designer chose that color for the display type?

10. Using the same pages from the previous exercise or other examples of unusual display type, consider why the designer chose that particular font for the display type.

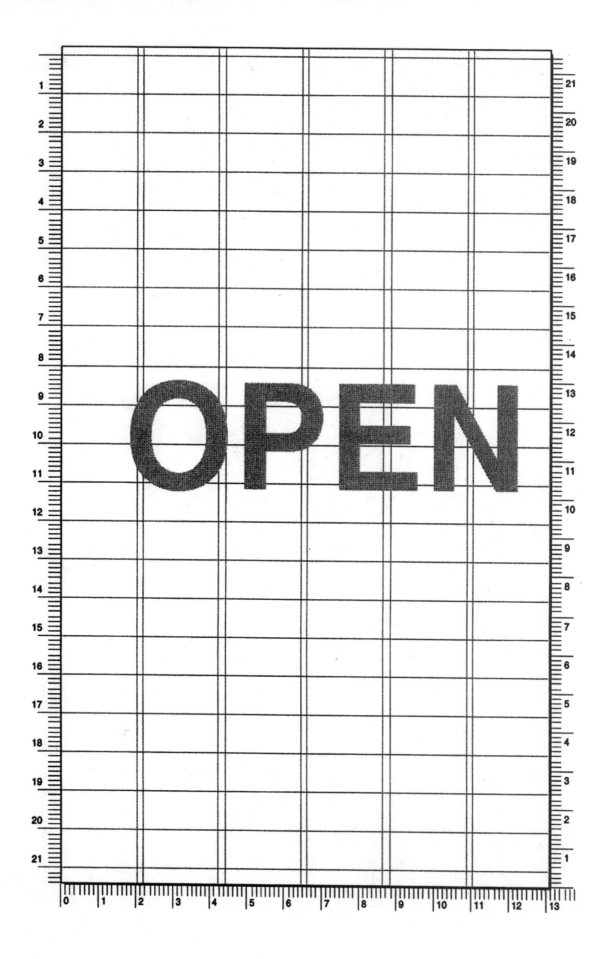

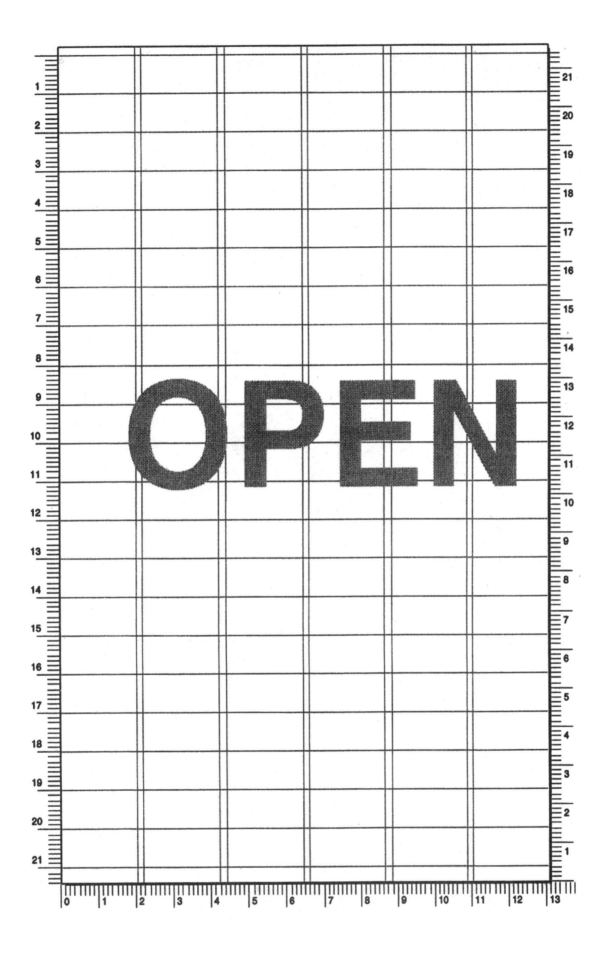

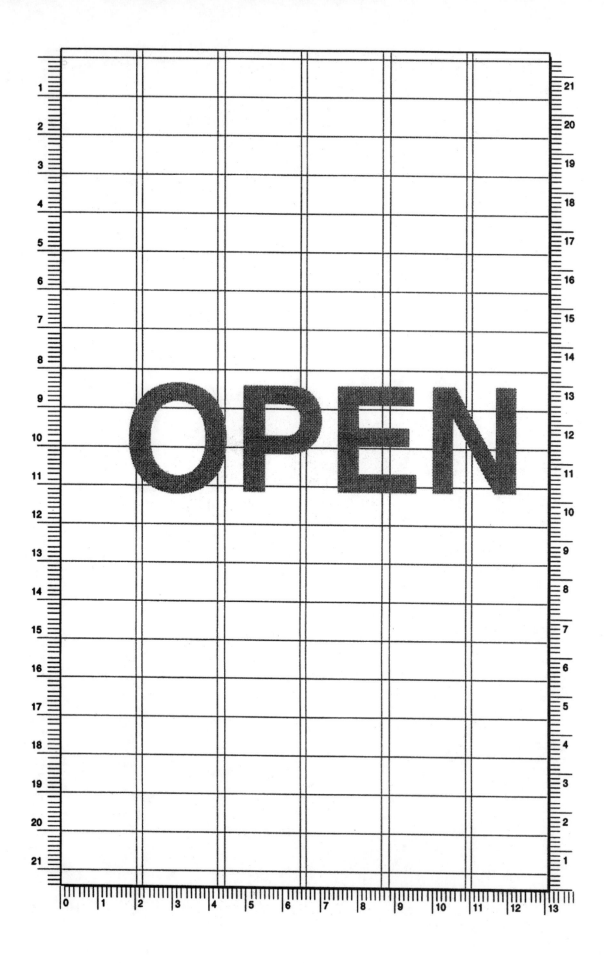

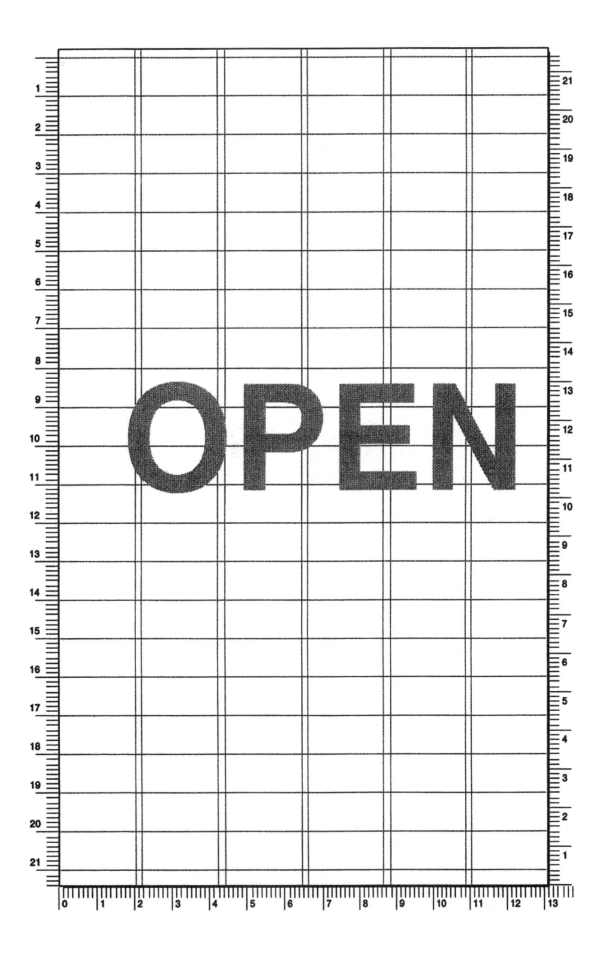

CHAPTER 16

From gatekeeper to guide: Editing for online media

The World Wide Web has emerged as a new medium in just a few years. There are many job opportunities, especially for those who combine journalism with a basic knowledge of computer coding. For several years, newspapers have retrained copy editors as Web editors. Now, positions at both newspapers and at Web-only enterprises are being filled directly. In either case, content is still the crucial element and readers still expect a publication to be free of errors. Thus, the role of copy editors is assured. But some of the duties of online copy editors are different from those of their traditional print counterparts.

One aspect of a Web editor's job is to take content that appears in the newspaper and prepare it for Web publication. But editing for the Web is, or should be, more than that. For example, the Web is all about making links — connections between a story on one Web site and related materials spread across the Web. Another aspect of Web editing is using the material available on the Web to strengthen a story you may be asked to work on for the print edition. Although the following exercises are not intended to turn you into a Web editor overnight, they should prepare you for some of the things a Web editor at a newspaper is required to do.

One caveat: If you are not already familiar with some of the conventions of the Web, now is a good time to learn some basics. This is not the place to get into the details of html coding, but you should be aware that the Web is a fast-changing medium. One of the most important warnings is that the links listed below may have died. And even if you can link to the site, some of its links may be dead. Sometimes you can revive a dead link by truncating the address. For example, if the address is www.somewhere.com/treasure/hunt.htm, and it's dead, try going to www.somewhere.com and seeing if you can drill down in the site to find the material. And since material is being added all the time, keeping up is a challenge. But competence at editing for the Web is one of the fastest-growing and most in-demand skills a journalist can have today.

Exercises

1. Look at the Web sites of various major metropolitan newspapers. Compare the way the sites are organized, whether searches are allowed and by what parameters, whether the newspaper archives are available online. Decide which site you like best and why. (If you are unsure of the Web address for a newspaper, use a search engine or go to www.newslink.org.)

2. Search the Web using words or phrases such as *editor*. Did you find anything useful? Bookmark any sites you might want to go back to.

3. Compare The New York Times Web site to the print version of the newspaper. Do the online stories mirror word-for-word the text of the printed version? Does the site have features that are omitted from

or impossible to produce in the printed version, such as links? Does the print version contain Web addresses? Should it?

4. Take from the daily newspaper a locally produced story that has a national or international angle, and see how much information you can find on the Web that could be used to expand, enhance or confirm information in the story. Do this by using one of the following widely recognized search engines. Now look up the same things using another search engine. Note the different sites each engine returns or fails to return. Not all search engines use the same techniques. (For a description of the attributes of various search engines, read the information provided at http://www.searchengineguide.org or http://www.powerreporting.com.)

   www.altavista.digital.com   www.lycos.com
   www.excite.com   www.northernlight.com
   www.hotbot.com   www.webcrawler.com
   www.infoseek.com   www.yahoo.com

   Also, you should do the same search using one of the metasearch engines:

   www.dogpile.com   www.mamma.com
   www.infind.com   www.metacrawler.com

5. Take a national story that appeared in a newspaper and add as many links as you can from it to Web sites for organizations mentioned in the news story. Try to find original documents the story mentions.

6. Develop a list of sites that you can use to check facts in stories while copy editing. These might include online phone books, crisscross directories, maps, corporate directories, encyclopedias, almanacs and fact books. If you need inspiration for sites to search for, just look for online versions of printed reference books you might use, such as a ZIP code directory. (Hint: Start at www.usps.gov.) Bookmark the sites you find useful. One site you should be sure to include is www.refdesk.com.

7. Because sites change constantly, you will need your own list of bookmarks. But bookmarks are not very useful unless they are organized in a logical way. Assuming you are on the national news desk, what links would you want to have, and how would you organize them? Do the same for another section of the newspaper, such as business or sports.

8. Find something interesting about your city or state at http://www.fedstats.gov.

9. What can you find out at http://www.mtnds.com/af/fr-top.asp?

Appendix

Spring Valley City Directory (Abridged)

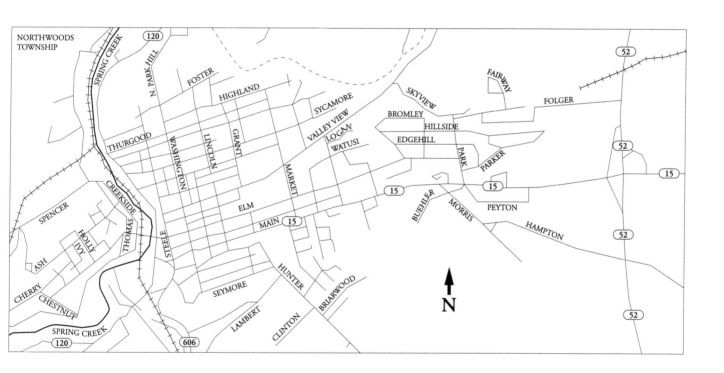

AAA Auto Sales 1630 E Hampton Av

Abrams Michael C 515 Bromley Rd

Abbott John & Lisa 403 Highland Av

Abdullah Marcus A 1513 Lambert St

Abramson Elliott 1211 Watusi Way

Accent on Hair 121 Main St

Achenbach Jonelle 704 Grant St

Adams Charles 14-A Thurgood La

A La Carte Catering 110 W Elm St

Alexander Timothy & Donna 501 Logan Way

Allen Bethany 807 Parker St

American Red Cross 204 Elm St

Anderson Paul 625 Hunter Av

Andrews Robert 158 Steele Dr

Antonucci Frank 1615-B Sycamore Pl

Aycock D 403 Lincoln St

Bannister Robert 212 Hunter Av

Bach JS 112 Highland Av

Barnes N 657 Ivy Way

Baxter Sean 225 Grant St

Bayshore Travel Agency 457 Foster St

Benton Barbara 805 Lambert St

Blain Anthony 312 Logan Way

Bloom Rosa 111 Valley View Dr

Brown Adelle 16 Fairway La

Brown Thomas 1465 Hillside Av

Buchanan Carla 511 Park Rd

Burns Adam 555 Steele Dr

Cable Martha 630 Holly St

Cain Michael 204 Valley View Dr

Calvary Baptist Church 658 Park Rd

Campanella George 432 Chestnut St

Campbell Glenn 1101 Park Rd

Cannon Richard & Susan 711 Cherry La

Carson Luther 120 Seymore St

Catherman Ruby 720 Creekside Dr

Chaffee B 612 Lambert St

Christopher M 445 Ash St

Chung Jong-Moon 1500 Hillside Av

Cohen Russell 105 Logan Way

Cole Stephen 1262 Peyton Pl

Crosby Douglas 738 Morris Rd

Davies Cecilia Sunnybrook Dairy Farm, P.O. Box 32, Northwoods Twp

Davis Matthew 215 Holly St

Days Inn 205 Main St

Dean James 501 Skyview Dr

Delacroix Sydney 25 Fairway La

Delmonico Gerald 220 Ash St

Deschamps W 515 Creekside Dr

Dix D 466 Cherry La

Dover Charles & Jane 3303 Morris Rd

Eastman G 215 Logan Way

Edmundson A 403 Edgehill Rd

Eisenhauer Katharine 1610 Hillside Av

Emerson David 320 Hunter Av

Empire Auto Works 1812 Morris Rd

Erickson Eric 545 Peyton Pl

Evans John 1205 Folger St

Fabiano A 1411 Market St

Fain Louise 214 Clinton St

Farnsworth G 349 Thomas Av

Faulkner Douglas 57 Washington St

First Presbyterian Church 1200 Morris Rd

Freeman Scott & Emily 413 Briarwood La

Funkhouser C 627 Spencer St

Gantt James 201 E Elm St

Gardner Asa 615 Foster St

Gonzalez Sgt Jesus 212 Edgehill Rd

Greene Suzanne mayor 106 Bromley Rd

Hagman Earle 1402-A Sycamore Pl

Hancock Kelly 101 Thomas Av

Hayes Emily & Randy Route One, Northwoods Twp

Henry Robert 358 Parker St

Hope Memorial Hospital 100 Market St

Kappelli Steven 225 Highland Av

Kennedy High School 819 Lincoln St

Knox Ed 450 Holly St

Langston David MD 202 Cherry La

Larkin Larry 513 Foster St

Lewis Karl & Marie 319 Edgehill Rd

Malloy Myrna 105 Clinton St

McBee Linda 501-B N Park Hill Rd

McCoy Funeral Home 102 E Elm St

McDonald's 360 W Elm St

McNichols Jon 511 Ivy Way

Moshowitz Howie 215 Briarwood La

Murphy Lt. Michael 220 Chestnut St

Newton Michael & Rebecca 608 Skyview Dr

Nichols Thomas 365 Clinton St

Norris David & Helen 738 Folger St

Old-Fashioned Churn 911 Buehler La

O'Riley Cpl Connor 103 Ash St

Our Lady of Hope RC Church 505 Chestnut St

Paradise Residential Care Center 101 Thomas Av

Park Hill Apartments N Park Hill Rd

Perkins Marla 538 Briarwood La

Potter Cynthia 111 Creekside Dr

Quattlebaum William & Edwina 312 Bromley Rd

Quik Stop 849 Buehler La

Quintero Carlos & Maria 305 Ash St

Redford James & Roberta 738 Ivy Way

Richards Sam 302-A North Park Hill Rd

Richardson Voncille 312 Skyview Dr

Rogers Neill & Stephanie 619 Peyton Pl

Ross Douglas & Carol 749 Spencer St

Rutledge Barnabas 426 Thomas Av

Sherrill Marc 214 Seymore St

Simms Bessie 3-D Sycamore Pl

Smith Kandy 525 Hunter Av

Spencer Charles & Caroline 520 Folger St

Stevens Andrew 612 Parker St

Sutherland David & Donna 324 Steele Dr

Symms Richard 3-G Thurgood La

Thomas John MD & Marcia 206 Valley View Dr

Thompson Myles 513 Holly St

Tomcyk Alexander 829 Peyton Pl

Turner Josiah & Bette 191 Parker St

Unger Stephen 854 Lincoln St

Underwood TW 714 Park Rd

Unitas Jonathan 356 Seymore St

United Way 314 Market St

Upchurch Gene & Lynn 410 Ivy Way

Urban Thomas & Gwen 559 Spencer St

Valmont Richard 212 Steele Dr

Veatch Russell 901 Valley View Dr

Wagoner Douglas & Anne 221 Thomas Av

Wainwright Cecil 203 Skyview Dr

Walker Frederick 22-C Thurgood La

Waller Aaron 304 Spencer St

Watson Col Gary 104 Fairway La

Welch Willard & Amy 213 Creekside Dr

White Rodger & Anita 410 Ash St

Williams Lance 420 Bromley Rd

Wood Nathan 612 Cherry La

Woodward Paul & Johanna 115 Chestnut St

Xu Li 513 Grant St

YMCA 516 Market St

Young Zachary 418 Seymore St

Zavaras Yiannis 319 Foster St

Zoloft Harry & Samantha 525 Ash St

Acknowledgments

Chapter 3
p. 7, "Embattled sex shops find a survival tactic works," New York Times Digest, October 19, 1998. Copyright © 1998 by The New York Times Company. Reprinted by permission. p. 8, © 1998 Associated Press. Reprinted by permission. p. 9, © 1998 Associated Press. Reprinted by permission. p. 10, Chris Gosier, "HealthSouth sues local man over Internet messages," Centre Daily Times, October 30, 1998. © 1998. Reprinted by permission of Knight Ridder.

Chapter 7
p. 64, "Sniper murders abortion doctor," by Carolyn Thompson, © 1998 Associated Press. Reprinted by permission. p. 66, "Abortion doctor in Buffalo slain; Sniper attack fits violent pattern," by Jim Yardley and David Rohde, The New York Times, October 25, 1998. Copyright © 1998 by The New York Times Company. Reprinted by permission. p. 70, "Israel to deport 11 cult members," by Charlie Brennan, Denver Rocky Mountain News, January 5, 1999. Copyright 1999. Reprinted by permission of the Denver Rocky Mountain News. p. 73, "Most cultists to be deported," by Peggy Lowe, Kevin Simpson, and Virginia Culver, The Denver Post, January 5, 1999. Copyright © 1999 Reprinted by permission. p. 77, "Survey: Teens drink, but don't drive," by Lindsey Tanner, © 1998 Associated Press. Reprinted by permission. p. 77, V. Dion Haynes, "Ranchers, authorities spar over wolves' return," Chicago Tribune, January 28, 1999. Reprinted with permission of Knight-Ridder/Tribune Information Services. p. 80, "Seeding shortage may hurt timber industry," by Dave Morantz, © 1999 Associated Press. Reprinted by permission.

Chapter 8
p. 84, Julie Cart and J.R. Moehringer, "Rowdy Denver fans revel in win: Super Bowl: Gridron glee spills into streets. Police move in to quash disturbances" Los Angeles Times, February 1, 1999. Copyright 1999 Los Angeles Times. Reprinted by permission. p. 87, "Deadly avalanches haunt the Alps," © 1999 Associated Press. Reprinted by permission. p. 89, Kurt Jensen, "Keillor stretches to pin parody on 'Big' bio," USA Today, March 4, 1999. Copyright 1999, Usa Today. Reprinted with permission. p. 96, "Worker killed, others hurt in explosion at Ford plant," © 1999 Associated Press. Reprinted by permission. p. 97, "O.J. Simpson auction to go online." © Reuters. Reprinted by permission. p. 98, Daniel Q. Haney, "Clot-dissolving medicine can reverse some strokes, study finds," Philadelphia Inquirer, February 5, 1999. © 1999. Reprinted by permission of the Associated Press. p. 100, Rochelle Hines, "Two executed in Oklahoma and Arizona," Philadelphia Inquirer, February 5, 1999. © 1999 Reprinted by permission of the Associated Press. P. 101, Tom Kirchofer, "In Boston, no appeal for school quotas," Philadelphia Inquirer, February 5, 1999. © 1999. Reprinted by permission of the Associated Press. p. 103, "Arafat says he wants to carry on peace accord," © 1999 Associated Press. Reprinted by permission. p. 104, "Families of cable car crash victims seeking compensation," © 1999 Associated Press. Reprinted by permission. p. 105, Elizabeth Olson, "A Swiss vote to legalize all drugs would save millions, backers say," New York Times, November 28, 1998. Copyright © 1998 by the New York Times Co. Reprinted with permission. p. 106, "Residents of West African nation flee," Philadelphia Inquirer, February 2, 1999. © 1999. Reprinted by permission of the Associated Press. p. 107, Anna Dolgov, "Space-Mirror trouble on Mir delays a test," Philadelphia Inquirer, February 5, 1999. © 1999. Reprinted by permission of the Associated Press.

Chapter 9
p. 109, "Pinned" by Mark Davis. Courtesy Philedelphia Inquirer. p. 112, "Smart part of the Web leads to trip down aisle and into People Magazine," by Margie Boulé. Courtesy The Oregonian. p. 115, "South rises again," by Sue Anne Pressley, The Washington Post, December 28, 1998. Copyright © 1999 The Washington Post. Reprinted by permission.

Chapter 10
p. 123, "Business" by Harry Zimbler. Pennsylvania Business Central. p. 125, John Schwartz, "Study uncovers bedroom blues," Washington Post, February 10, 1999. © 1999, The Washington Post. Reprinted with permission. p. 128, "Poll finds Americans feel loss of health care control," © 1999 Associated Press. Reprinted by permission.

Chapter 12
p. 139, © 1998 Associated Press. Reprinted with permission. p. 140, "As California contains fire, focus shifts to flood peril," Associated Press, October 25, 1998. © Associated Press. Reprinted by permission. p. 140, "California seeks new limits on boat pollution," Associated Press, October 25, 1998. © 1998 Associated Press. Reprinted with permission. p. 142, Kevin Hoffman, "Two studies shed light on cancer in women," Associated Press, October 1, 1998. © 1998 Associated Press. Reprinted with permission. p. 144, Karen Lee Ziner, "Pet put tight squeeze on its owner," Providence Journal, October 16, 1998. © 1998. Reprinted by permission. p. 146, "Alcohol a factor in Johnston collision that killed four," by Demorris Lee, The News & Observer, December 30, 1998. © 1999. Reprinted by permission of The News & Observer of Raleigh, North Carolina.

Pour docteur S[...]

Kaoru
Shimamoto

le 19 novembre ..6

気軽に楽しむ

タルト大好き!

J'adore les tartes !

島本 薫
Kaoru Shimamoto

文化出版局

プロローグ　4

Part1
Tarte de base
まずは基本のタルト生地の作り方から　6

パート・シュクレ　7

Sommaire

Part2
Desserts et goûters au quotidien
日々のおやつとデザート　11

〈パート・シュクレ生地を使って〉
ママンの簡単いちごタルト　12
三温糖のタルト　14
コーヒーのタルト　16
ショコラ&オレンジのタルト　18
りんご&シナモンのタルト　20
チェリー&ピスタチオのクランブルタルト　22
マロンクリーム&和栗の渋皮煮タルト　24
アプリコットのクランブルタルト　26
ダコワーズ&いちごのタルト　28

〈パート・ブリゼ・シュクレ生地を使って〉
りんごの簡単タルト　30
ピスタチオ&プティ・ポワールのタルト　32
ピスタチオ&グレープフルーツのタルト　34
クレーム&ブラックベリーのタルト　36
タルト・オ・シトロン　38
チェリークラフティのタルト　40
ココナッツ&パイナップルのタルト　42
ココア&プルーン&ナッツのタルト　44
抹茶&茶福豆のタルト　46

パート・ブリゼ(シュクレ、サレ)　48
イタリアン・メレンゲ　51

Part 3
Pour entrée et plat principal

52 前菜やメインに

〈パート・ブリゼ・サレ生地を使って〉

- **54** グリーンアスパラガス&スモークサーモンのキッシュ
- **56** きのこのキッシュ
- **58** キッシュ・ロレーヌ
- **60・62** そら豆&グリーンピースのキッシュ+にんじんサラダ
- **61・63** チーズフォンデュのタルト
- **64・66** 炒め玉ねぎ&じゃがいも&カマンベールのタルト
- **65・67** 南仏野菜のキッシュ

Part 4
Préparer autrement les pâtes restantes

68 2番生地を使ってアレンジ

- **68・70** 抹茶のミルフイユ
- **69・71** 4種類のアイスクリームとともに
- **72・74** フリュイ・ルージュ+クレーム・パティシエール
- **73・75** グラスデザート2種
- **76・78** ブリゼ・サレ・スティック（プレーン、黒ごま、パルメザン）、タラマ
- **77・79** ディップ4種
- **80・82** スモークサーモンのサラダ+バルサミコドレッシング
- **81・83** 完熟トマトのピッツァ、サーモンのリエット、アヴォカド+えび

・この本で使用している
　計量単位は、1カップ=200ml、
　大さじ1=15ml、小さじ1=5mlです。
・この本に表示されている
　「塩　ひとつまみ」は、
　親指と人さし指でつまんだ量（約0.5g）です。
・卵はLサイズ、バターは食塩不使用のものを
　使用しています。
・この本では、
　家庭用の電気オーブンを使用しています。
　温度、焼き時間は、
　オーブンの種類や大きさによって
　異なりますので、目安としてください。

J'adore les tartes!

プロローグ

フランス滞在中、友人宅でいちばんよく口にしたお菓子は「タルト」でした。フランスの友人たちが作るそれは、陶器の型にバターをぬって、めん棒を使わずに手でじかに生地をのばして焼き、ジャムをぬった上にフルーツをのせたり、クラフティ生地と季節のフルーツを入れて焼くなど、驚くほどに簡単でダイナミックなものでした。スーパーでものばした生地が売られていますし、お菓子作りから程遠いイメージのエリート男性だって、手際よく作ったりするのです。フランス人にとってタルトは、がんばった自分へのご褒美や、特別な人を招くときのためのものではなく、食事の後のデザートに、または、ちょっと甘いものが食べたいとき、気が置けない友人を食事に招くときなど、気軽に口にする日常のお菓子なのです。生地を均一にのばさなくては、などと神経質になって作っていた私でしたが、それを知ってからは、気軽に楽しめるようになりました。この本では、皆さまにお菓子作りに成功していただくために、私のレシピを詳しくお伝えし、アパレイユを残さないよう、分量の単位は細かい区切りとなっています。また、同じお菓子でも、小さく作るよりも、大きく作ったほうが味がいいため、大きいタイプのタルトをご紹介しています。どうぞ皆さまも肩の力を抜いて、「タルトの世界」を気軽にお楽しみいただければ幸いです。

Part I
まずは基本のタルト生地の作り方から
Tarte de base

タルト生地には、型抜きクッキーのような歯ざわりの「パート・シュクレ」と、
折りパイのような歯ざわりの「パート・ブリゼ」があり、
アパレイユ、具材を含めた全体のバランスによって、どちらを使うかを決めます。
生地作りから、から焼きまで、簡単な作業ですが、
おいしく仕上げるコツをご紹介しましょう。

パート・シュクレ
Pâte sucrée

カリッとした歯ざわりと香ばしさが身上の「パート・シュクレ」。しっかりとから焼きしましょう。

材料
(基本量・直径20cmのタルト型1台分)
バター　65g
粉糖　28g
塩　ひとつまみ
全卵　17g
薄力粉　125g
強力粉(打ち粉用)　適宜
全卵(ドレ用)　適宜

準備
- バターは室温に戻しておく（指で押してみて軽くへこむ程度。やわらかくしすぎない。小さなさいころ状にしておくと早く室温に戻る）。
- 粉糖はふるっておく。
- クッキングシートを1/6に折り、型の底面の半径＋高さ＋4cmの長さを残して切り、切り口の真ん中に約4cmの切れ目を入れる［写真14］。
- 型はペーパータオルを使ってバターを薄くぬる［写真15］。
- オーブンを180℃に温める。

作り方
ボウルにバターを入れ、ハンドミキサーで軽く混ぜたら、粉糖、塩を加え、ハンドミキサーでバターがなめらかになるまで混ぜる。

2 1にときほぐした全卵を3回に分けて加え、そのつど卵がバターにしっかりとなじむまで混ぜる。

3 2に薄力粉をふるいにかけながら加え、ボウルをときどき回しながらカードをボウルの中で前後させ、生地全体を軽くなじませる(生地は粉っぽい状態。室温が高いときは、冷蔵庫で休ませる)。

4 3を両手でギュッと握って台の上に重ねて置き、手のひらの腹で、生地を台にすりつけながら向う側に移動させる(生地全体をなじませるため)。ひととおり移動したら、カードで生地をひとまとめにし、ラップで包んで平らにして、冷蔵庫で1時間から一晩休ませる(焼縮みを少なくするため、一晩休ませるのが理想)。

5 生地を2回折りたたみ、手のひらでギュッと押さえ、なじんだら球状に丸める（ひび割れを防ぐため）。

6 台とめん棒に打ち粉をふり（ふりすぎると生地がボソボソになる。打ち粉は最小限に）、めん棒を軽く動かしながら、生地が4mm厚さになるまで少しずつのばす（ときどき生地の向きを変え、くっつくようなら打ち粉をする）。

7 生地に型を当て、大きさ（底面＋高さ＋α）が充分かどうかを確認したら、生地についた打ち粉をはけで払い、生地を型の上にふんわりとのせる。

8 生地の端を両手で持ち、下に向かって押し込むようにしながら一周し、型からはみ出た部分を外に向かって折る。型の上にめん棒を転がして、余分な生地を切り落とす。

9 親指と人さし指で側面を挟みながら一周する（生地が足りないところは残り生地で補整する）。残り生地を丸めて側面部を押さえながら一周し、生地を型に密着させる。

10 フォークで生地の底面に穴をあけ（これをピケといい、底にたまった空気の抜け口となる。ピケをしないと底面の生地がふくれ上がる。液状のアパレイユを流すときは、穴を下まで貫通させずに表面にだけ穴をあける）、冷蔵庫で20分休ませる。

11 10の上に準備したクッキングシートを敷き込み、重しを入れる。シートをしっかりと側面に沿わせ、縁のほうが多くなるように重しを調節する。

12 あらかじめ熱しておいたオーブンで20分焼き、重しを取って、ときほぐした全卵をはけで側面と底にぬって（これをドレといい、生地をコーティングする役目がある。水分の多いアパレイユを流すときは、念入りに）、さらに約10分焼き、型に入れたまま網の上で冷ます（から焼きした後、充分に冷ますことにより、タルト台のカリッと感をより長もちさせることができる）。

＊生地は直径20cmの型1台分を目安としているが、ぎりぎりの量なので、敷き込みにくい場合は2台分で作業を行なう。

＊重しは重量感があり、熱伝導のいいタルトストーンがおすすめ。

＊生地の保存は冷蔵庫で約3日、冷凍庫で約1か月。まとめて作って密封し、冷凍しておくと便利。解凍は室温または冷蔵庫で。

Part 2
日々のおやつとデザート
Desserts et goûters au quotidien

タルト台をから焼きしたら、中身を作りましょう。
日常の素朴なタルトは、混ぜて、流して、焼くだけ。
ちょっとがんばって作るおめかしタルトは、特別な日のデザートやプレゼントに。
アパレイユの焼上りの目安は、竹串を刺して、生地がくっついてこなければOK。

〈パート・シュクレ生地を使って〉
ママンの簡単いちごタルト
Tarte aux fraises maison

これがプロローグに登場した、フランス人お得意の「お気軽タルト」。市販のジャムを使えば、よりいっそう簡単にできます。ジャムと果物はお好みの組合せで、季節の果物をふんだんにのせて召し上がれ。お気楽な私は、型にバターをぬらずにから焼きしたら、タルト生地が型にくっついて取れなくなりました……。ご注意ください。

材料
（直径18cmの陶製タルト型1台分）
パート・シュクレ(p.7参照)　基本量
いちご　適宜

ルバーブジャムの材料
ルバーブ（冷凍）　230g
グラニュー糖　80g
＊ルバーブはペーパータオルの上で表面の霜をとかしてから計量する。

冷凍ルバーブは、インターネット通販などで入手できます。
インターネット通販「クオカ」
http://www.cuoca.com

準備
- ルバーブにグラニュー糖をまぶして、ルバーブから水分が出るまで室温でおいておく。
- p.7と同様にして型を準備する。

作り方

1 準備したルバーブを強火にかけ、沸騰したらあくを取り、弱火にして煮る。ルバーブがやわらかくなったらスプーンで繊維をほぐしながら煮て、軽くとろみがついたら火から下ろす。完全に冷めたら冷蔵庫で冷やす。

2 パート・シュクレを作り、型に生地を直接のばし、ピケ（多数）をして、から焼きする（p.7～10参照。重しを取った後、ドレをして、さらに約20分焼く）。

3 タルト台にルバーブジャムを詰め、いちごを並べる。あれば、いちごの花や葉を飾る。

食べごろ：当日・冷やして

〈パート・シュクレ生地を使って〉
三温糖のタルト
Tarte au sucre

初めてフランス人宅の夕食に招かれたときのデザートが、このタルトでした。中身がプリンに似ていて、素朴で懐かしい味わいに、お代りまでしてしまった食いしん坊な私。もともとは、台がタルトではなく、発酵生地を使った地方菓子「タルト・オ・シュークル」をアレンジしたものだそう。それをまた私なりにアレンジしてみました。

材料
(直径18cmの陶製タルト型1台分)
パート・シュクレ(p.7参照) 基本量
全卵 140g
三温糖 75g
牛乳 95ml
粉糖(飾り用) 適宜

準備
・p.7と同様にして型を準備する。
・三温糖はふるっておく。
・オーブンを170℃に温める。

作り方

1. パート・シュクレを作り、ピケをしないでから焼きする(p.7～10参照。タルト台の底がふくらんだら、表面をやさしく押さえて、入ったひびにドレをして、オーブンで約1分乾かす)。

2. ボウルに全卵を入れて泡立て器でときほぐし、三温糖を加えて、三温糖が溶けるまで混ぜたら、牛乳を加え、泡立て器でなじませる。

3. タルト台に**2**をこし器でこしながら入れ、オーブンで約35分焼き、粗熱が取れたら型ごと冷蔵庫で冷やし、表面に粉糖をふりかけていただく。

食べごろ：1～2日目　冷やして

〈パート・シュクレ生地を使って〉
コーヒーのタルト
Tarte au café

フランスでは、フランス人主婦主宰の様々な料理教室に通っていました。このタルトは、その一人、Dauder先生に教えていただいた「くるみの粉」を使ったタルトをアレンジしたもの。ナイフを入れると、切り口は茶色のグラデーションが美しく、コーヒーのいい香りが漂います。インスタントコーヒーは、お好みのものをお使いください。

パート・シュクレ・カカオの材料

（直径20cmのタルト型1台分）
バター　65g
粉糖　28g
塩　ひとつまみ
全卵　17g
薄力粉　120g
ココア　8g
＊薄力粉をふるいにかけ、ココアを目の細かい茶こしでふるい入れて、よく混ぜ合わせて使用する。

タルトの材料

全卵　60g
卵黄　20g
グラニュー糖　68g
インスタントコーヒー　4g
湯　128ml
アーモンドパウダー　68g
薄力粉　4g
＊インスタントコーヒーはネスカフェのゴールドブレンドを使用。

準備

・p.7と同様にして型を準備する。
・アーモンドパウダー、薄力粉は合わせてふるっておく。
・オーブンを150℃に温める。

作り方

1 パート・シュクレ・カカオを作り、ピケをしないで、から焼きする（p.7～10参照）。

2 ボウルに全卵、卵黄を入れて泡立て器でときほぐし、グラニュー糖を加えて、グラニュー糖が溶けるまで混ぜる。

3 インスタントコーヒーを湯で溶かし、熱いうちに**2**に加えて、泡立て器でなじませる。

4 **3**に粉類を加えて泡立て器でなじませたら、タルト台に流し入れ、オーブンで約40分焼き、粗熱が取れたら型ごと冷蔵庫で冷やす。

食べごろ：1～2日目　冷やして

この本では主に、
直径20×高さ2.6cmの円形の型、
24.7×10×高さ2.4cmの長方形の型
（どちらも底が取れるもの）を
使用しています。
メーカーによって、
容量や縁の角度が多少異なります。

〈パート・シュクレ生地を使って〉
ショコラ&オレンジのタルト
Tarte au chocolat et aux oranges

ショコラとオレンジの相性がいいのは周知のこと。でも大好きなので、パウンドケーキに続く第2弾。ビターなココアのタルト台に、砂糖を極限まで減らした生チョコのようなとろける生地、ジューシーで色鮮やかなオレンジ。とっても贅沢で大人の味わい。グルメで有名な知人に差し上げたら、ご家族中で取合いになったそう。光栄です。

パート・シュクレ・カカオの材料
（約25×10×高さ2.5cmのタルト型1台分）
バター　65g
粉糖　28g
塩　ひとつまみ
全卵　17g
薄力粉　120g
ココア　8g
＊薄力粉をふるいにかけ、ココアを目の細かい茶こしでふるい入れて、よく混ぜ合わせて使用する。

タルトの材料
オレンジ　7切れ（約1個分）
全卵　40g
卵黄　12g
グラニュー糖　25g
生クリーム　78ml
チョコレート　65g
＊チョコレートは酸味のあるヴァローナのManjari/マンジャリ（カカオ64％）を使用。

準備
- p.7と同様にして型を準備する。
- チョコレートは細かく刻んでおく（コインタイプのものはそのままで）。
- オーブンを180℃に温める。

作り方
1 パート・シュクレ・カカオを作り、ピケをしないで、から焼きする（p.7〜10参照）。オレンジの果肉を取り出して、ざるに並べて水分をきる（p.35参照）。

2 ボウルに全卵、卵黄を入れて泡立て器でときほぐし、グラニュー糖を加えて、グラニュー糖が溶けるまで混ぜる。

3 小鍋に生クリームを入れて、鍋の縁が沸騰するまで温める。チョコレートを耐熱容器に入れて、電子レンジにかけてとかし（半量がとけるくらい。沸騰させない）、生クリームを加えてスプーンで混ぜてなじませる。

4 2に3を加え、ゴムべらでよく混ぜ合わせたら、タルト台に流し入れ、オレンジを重ならないように並べて、オーブンで約25分焼き、粗熱が取れたら、型から出して網の上で冷ます。

食べごろ：1〜2日目　冷やして

〈パート・シュクレ生地を使って〉
りんご&シナモンのタルト
Tarte aux pommes et à la cannelle

パリ7区の「マルシェ・サックス・ブルトゥイユ」においしいりんご屋さんが出店していたので、住んでいた16区からメトロに乗ってよく買いに行ったものです。近所の八百屋さんのものと違って、酸味と甘さのバランスがよく、みつのような味わいに心ひかれました。このタルトに使うりんごは、紅玉など、酸味のあるものがおすすめです。

材料

(直径20cmのタルト型1台分)
パート・シュクレ(p.7参照)　基本量
アーモンドパウダー　50g
グラニュー糖　62g
全卵　83g
薄力粉　39g
ベーキングパウダー　1g(小さじ1/2)
シナモンパウダー　1.5g(小さじ3/4)
バター　25g
りんご　正味90g(約1/2個分)
グラニュー糖(飾り用)　10g
シナモンパウダー(飾り用)　ひとつまみ

準備

- p.7と同様にして型を準備する。
- アーモンドパウダーはふるっておく。
- 薄力粉、ベーキングパウダーを合わせてふるい、シナモンパウダーを目の細かい茶こしでふるい入れて、よく混ぜ合わせておく。
- 飾り用のグラニュー糖とシナモンパウダーはよく混ぜ合わせておく。
- オーブンを180℃に温める。

作り方

1. パート・シュクレを作り、ピケ(多数)をして、から焼きする(p.7～10参照)。
2. りんごは縦1/4に切って皮をむいて芯を取る。それをさらに縦1/2に切って1.5cm厚さのいちょう切りにする。
3. ボウルにアーモンドパウダー、グラニュー糖を入れ、全卵を加えて、泡立て器で白っぽくなるまで混ぜる。
4. 3に粉類を加え、ゴムべらですくい上げるようにして粉類が見えなくなるまで混ぜ、とかしバターをゴムべらに伝わせながら加えて、バターが見えなくなるまで混ぜる。
5. タルト台に4を流して、りんごを表面にのせるように並べ、混ぜ合わせておいたグラニュー糖とシナモンパウダーをふりかけて、オーブンで約35分焼き、粗熱が取れたら、型から出して網の上で冷ます。

食べごろ：2～3日目　冷やして

〈パート・シュクレ生地を使って〉
チェリー&ピスタチオのクランブルタルト
Tarte crumble à la pistache et aux cerises

フランスでピスタチオを買ったら、1kg入りしかなくて、なかなか使いきれず、粒のままサラダにふりかけたり、おつまみのピーナッツのようにポリポリとかじったりしていました。でもあまりにも贅沢だと反省し、誕生したのがこのタルトと『パウンドケーキ大好き』でご紹介したケーキでした。ピスタチオ好きにはたまらないお菓子です。

材料
（約25×10×高さ2.5cmのタルト型1台分）
パート・シュクレ（p.7参照）　基本量
ピスタチオ（皮なし）　25g
粉糖　37g
全卵　45g
薄力粉　20g
ベーキングパウダー　0.5g（小さじ¼）
バター　15g
アメリカンダークチェリー（缶詰）　24個

クランブルの材料
ピスタチオ（皮なし）　38g
粉糖　18g
グラニュー糖　10g
薄力粉　20g
バター　20g

クランブルの準備
・ピスタチオは粉糖とともにフードプロセッサーにかけ、粉状にしてふるっておく（生地用も同様に）。
・薄力粉はふるっておく。
・バターは8mm角に切って、使う直前まで冷蔵庫に入れておく。

クランブルの作り方
ボウルにバター以外の材料を入れ、均一になるように泡立て器で混ぜる。バターを加えてカードで刻み、バターを粉類とともに指先でつぶす。材料がなじんだら、手でギュッと握って固め、冷蔵庫で冷やす（p.26参照）。

タルトの準備
・p.7と同様にして型を準備する。
・チェリーはペーパータオルの上でしっかりと水分をきっておく。
・薄力粉、ベーキングパウダーは合わせてふるっておく。
・オーブンを180℃に温める。

タルトの作り方
1　パート・シュクレを作り、ピケ（多数）をして、から焼きする（p.7～10参照）。
2　ボウルに合わせて粉状にしたピスタチオと粉糖を入れ、全卵を加えて、泡立て器で粉糖が溶けるまで混ぜる。
3　2に粉類を加え、ゴムべらですくい上げるようにして粉類が見えなくなるまで混ぜ、とかしバターをゴムべらに伝わせながら加えて、バターが見えなくなるまで混ぜる。
4　タルト台に3を流してチェリーを並べ、クランブル生地を粗くくずして表面に散らし、オーブンで約40分焼いて、粗熱が取れたら型から出して網の上で冷ます。

食べごろ：2日目　冷やして

〈パート・シュクレ生地を使って〉
マロンクリーム&和栗の渋皮煮タルト
Tarte aux marrons français et japonais

隣人だったフランソワーズは、パリ・セレブが集まるサロン・ドゥ・テによく連れていってくれました。そこで出会った「栗のケーキ」は絶品で、再現しようと試みたのですが、いまだ完成せず……。でも、そのとき生み出したお菓子が、このタルトの中身。外見は地味ですが、日仏の栗をふんだんに使い、リッチな味わいに仕上がりました。

材料

(直径20cmのタルト型1台分)
- パート・シュクレ(p.7参照)　基本量
- クレーム・ドゥ・マロン　65g
- バター　45g
- 薄力粉　9g
- 卵白(メレンゲ用)　57g
- グラニュー糖(メレンゲ用)　16g
- 卵黄　36g
- グラニュー糖　16g
- 和栗の渋皮煮(市販品)　80g

準備
- p.7と同様にして型を準備する。
- 薄力粉はふるっておく。
- 栗はペーパータオルの上でしっかりと水分をきってから、好みの大きさに切る。
- オーブンを170℃に温める。

作り方

1 パート・シュクレを作り、ピケ(多数)をして、から焼きする(p.7～10参照)。

2 小さなボウルにクレーム・ドゥ・マロンを入れ、とかしバターを加えて泡立て器でなじませたら、薄力粉を加え、薄力粉が見えなくなるまで泡立て器で混ぜる。

3 別のボウルに卵白を入れて、ハンドミキサーでしっかりと泡立てたら、グラニュー糖を2回に分けて加え、角がピンと立つまで泡立てる。

4 別のボウルに卵黄とグラニュー糖を入れて(ハンドミキサーについたメレンゲを軽く落として、洗わずに使用する)、グラニュー糖が溶けるまでハンドミキサーで混ぜる。

5 2に4の1/2量を加えて泡立て器でしっかりとなじませ、4のボウルに戻し、生地を持ち上げるようにして、泡立て器を一か所で回転させながらボウルを手前に回して、やさしくなじませる。

6 5にメレンゲの1/2量を加えて泡立て器でしっかりとなじませ、メレンゲのボウルに戻し、5と同様にして混ぜる。

7 タルト台に栗をまんべんなく散らし、6を流してオーブンで約40分焼き、粗熱が取れたら型から出して網の上で冷ます。

食べごろ：2～3日目　冷やして

〈パート・シュクレ生地を使って〉
アプリコットのクランブルタルト
Tarte crumble aux abricots

クランブルはもともとイギリスのものですが、今ではフランス家庭にすっかりなじんでいます。本来は、耐熱容器の中に季節の果物を入れ、その上に散らしてオーブンで焼くのですが、今回はタルトにしてみました。クランブルは冷凍で約1か月保存ができ、解凍せずに使えます。おいしく仕上げるコツは、細かくくずしすぎないこと。

材料
（直径20cmのタルト型1台分）
パート・シュクレ（p.7参照）　基本量
アーモンドパウダー　25g
グラニュー糖　35g
全卵　45g
薄力粉　20g
ベーキングパウダー　0.5g（小さじ¼）
バター　15g
アプリコット（缶詰・半割り）　12個

クランブルの材料
アーモンドパウダー　40g
薄力粉　20g
三温糖　28g
バター　20g

クランブルの準備
- 粉類、三温糖は合わせてふるっておく。
- バターは8mm角に切って直前まで冷蔵庫に入れておく。

クランブルの作り方
ボウルにバター以外の材料を入れ、均一になるように泡立て器で混ぜる。バターを加えてカードで刻み、バターを粉類とともに指先でつぶす。材料がなじんだら、手でギュッと握って固め、冷蔵庫で冷やす。

タルトの準備
- p.7と同様にして型を準備する。
- アプリコットはペーパータオルの上でしっかりと水分をきっておく。
- アーモンドパウダーはふるっておく。
- 薄力粉、ベーキングパウダーは合わせてふるっておく。
- オーブンを180℃に温める。

タルトの作り方
1. パート・シュクレを作り、ピケ（多数）をして、から焼きする（p.7〜10参照）。
2. ボウルにアーモンドパウダー、グラニュー糖を入れ、全卵を加えて、泡立て器で白っぽくなるまで混ぜる。
3. 2に粉類を加え、ゴムべらですくい上げるようにして粉類が見えなくなるまで混ぜ、とかしバターをゴムべらに伝わせながら加えて、バターが見えなくなるまで混ぜる。
4. タルト台に3を流してアプリコットを並べ、クランブル生地を粗くくずして表面に散らし、オーブンで約40分焼いて、粗熱が取れたら型から出して網の上で冷ます。

食べごろ：1〜2日目　冷やして

〈パート・シュクレ生地を使って〉
ダコワーズ&いちごのタルト
Tarte à la dacquoise et aux fraises

かめばかむほど味が出る、スルメのような?ダコワーズ。私のレシピは、アーモンドパウダーをふんだんに使い、濃厚な味わいが特徴。コーヒー味のバタークリームやショコラ・ガナッシュとともにいただくのも好きですが、フレッシュな果物を添えるのもいいものです。混ぜ方が足りないと、生地がしぼんでしまうので注意しましょう。

材料
(直径20cmのタルト型1台分)
パート・シュクレ(p.7参照)　基本量
卵白(メレンゲ用)　96g
グラニュー糖(メレンゲ用)　24g
アーモンドパウダー　96g
粉糖　75g
薄力粉　16g
ピスタチオ(皮なし)　8g
いちご　適宜
粉糖(飾り用)　適宜

準備
- p.7と同様にして型を準備する。
- アーモンドパウダー、粉糖、薄力粉は合わせてふるい、よく混ぜ合わせておく。
- ピスタチオは粗く刻んでおく。
- オーブンを180℃に温める。

作り方
1. パート・シュクレを作り、ピケ(多数)をして、から焼きする(p.7〜10参照)。
2. ボウルに卵白を入れて、ハンドミキサーでしっかりと泡立てたら、グラニュー糖を3回に分けて加え、角がピンと立つまで泡立てる。
3. 2に粉類を2回に分けて加え、ゴムべらで生地を持ち上げるようにして生地につやと粘りが出るまでしっかりと混ぜて(初めは混ざりにくいが、メレンゲが見えなくなるまで気長に混ぜる)、直径1cmの丸口金をつけた絞出し袋に入れる。
4. タルト台に3を中央から外へ渦巻き状に絞り、半量のピスタチオを散らす。2段目は中央に直径6cmのスペースをあけて、1段目と同様に絞り、残りのピスタチオを散らす。
5. 4に粉糖を2回ふりかけて、180℃のオーブンで20分焼き、さらに170℃で約20分焼いて、粗熱が取れたら型から出して冷蔵庫で冷やし、いちごを飾って供する。

食べごろ：2〜3日目　冷やして

〈パート・ブリゼ・シュクレ生地を使って〉
りんごの簡単タルト
Tarte très facile aux pommes

友人ベルトランがデザートに作ってくれたのが、このタルト。天板に直接生地を置くので、型いらずでとっても簡単。しかもおいしいのでおすすめです。りんご、いちじく、アプリコットなど生の果物を薄くスライスしてのせるだけ。縁を折り曲げると、そこがサクッと焼き上がって美味。焼きたてでも、冷やしても、どちらでも楽しめます。

パート・ブリゼ・シュクレ・アマンドの材料

（約6人分）
薄力粉　110g
アーモンドパウダー　15g
グラニュー糖　25g
塩　1g
バター　60g
全卵　32g
水　3ml
＊薄力粉とアーモンドパウダーを合わせてふるっておく。

タルトの材料

りんご　½個
カソナード、またはグラニュー糖　10g
バター　10g
＊りんごは紅玉など酸味のあるものがおすすめです。

準備
・オーブンを180℃に温める。

作り方

1　パート・ブリゼ・シュクレ・アマンドを作り（p.48〜50参照）、5mm厚さにのばしてピケ（多数）をする。

2　りんごは皮をむいて、円形の抜き型などで芯を取り、横3mm厚さに切る。

3　天板にクッキングシートを敷き、生地をのせてりんごを並べる。カソナードと小さく切ったバターを散らして、生地の縁を内側に折り、オーブンで約35分焼く。

食べごろ：当日　焼きたて、粗熱を取って、冷やして

〈パート・ブリゼ・シュクレ生地を使って〉
ピスタチオ&プティ・ポワールのタルト
Tarte à la pistache et aux petites poires

ピスタチオは、グリーンが鮮やかでパンチのある味わいのイラン産と、甘みのあるイタリアのシチリア産のものを使い分けています。この本で使用しているのは前者ですが、インターネット通販でも入手することができます。プティ・ポワールは、ビジュアル面を重視して使用しましたが、ご家庭では一般的な洋梨缶がおすすめです。

材料

（約25×10×高さ2.5cmのタルト型1台分）
パート・ブリゼ・シュクレ（p.48参照） 基本量
バター　45g
グラニュー糖　25g
ピスタチオ（皮なし）　27g
粉糖　20g
アーモンドパウダー　27g
全卵　30g
ピスタチオ（皮なし・飾り用）　6g
プティ・ポワール（缶詰）　5個
グラサージュ（飾り用）　適宜
＊グラサージュの代りに、
アプリコットジャムを湯でのばして使ってもいい。
＊プティ・ポワールの代りに、
並サイズのポワールを、
薄くスライスして並べてもいい。
＊プティ・ポワールやグラサージュは
インターネット通販「クオカ」で入手可（p.12参照）。

準備

- p.7と同様にして型を準備する。
- バターは室温に戻しておく（指で押してみて軽くへこむ程度。やわらかくしすぎない。小さなさいころ状にしておくと早く室温に戻る）。
- 飾り用を除くピスタチオと粉糖をフードプロセッサーにかけて細かくし、アーモンドパウダーと一緒にふるっておく。
- プティ・ポワールは、ペーパータオルの上でしっかりと水分をきり、底を平らになるように切っておく。
- 飾り用のピスタチオは好みの大きさに刻んでおく。
- オーブンを170℃に温める。

作り方

1 パート・ブリゼ・シュクレを作り、ピケ（多数）をして、から焼きする（p.48～50参照）。

2 ボウルにバターとグラニュー糖を入れ、ハンドミキサーでバターがもったりとして白っぽくなるまで混ぜる。

3 2に粉類を加え、ハンドミキサーで軽くなじませたら、全卵をよくときほぐして2～3回に分けて加え（しっかりとなじんでから次を加える）、ハンドミキサーでよく混ぜる。

4 3を直径1cmの丸口金をつけた絞出し袋に入れ、タルト台に絞って表面をスプーンで平らにし、飾り用のピスタチオをまんべんなく散らして、プティ・ポワールを埋め込み、オーブンで約55分焼く。

5 粗熱が取れたら、表面全体にグラサージュをはけでぬり、型から出して網の上で冷ます。

食べごろ：1～2日目　冷やして

〈パート・ブリゼ・シュクレ生地を使って〉
ピスタチオ&グレープフルーツのタルト
Tarte à la pistache et aux pamplemousses

テレビの取材で、タレントさんにこのタルトをお教えしたら、かなりの反響がありました。ピスタチオとグレープフルーツの組合せは、フランスでは珍しいことではないのですが、大部分のパティスリーがピスタチオペーストを使っているようです。このレシピは、ピスタチオそのものを使用するので、やはり味と香りが違います。

材料

（約25×10×高さ2.5cmのタルト型1台分）
パート・ブリゼ・シュクレ（p.48参照）　基本量
グレープフルーツ（ルビー）　約1½個
バター　45g
グラニュー糖　25g
ピスタチオ（皮なし）　27g
粉糖　20g
アーモンドパウダー　27g
全卵　30g
グランマルニエ　4ml
グラサージュ（飾り用）　適宜
ピスタチオ（皮なし・飾り用）　6g
＊グラサージュの代りに、
アプリコットジャムを湯でのばして使ってもいい。

準備

- p.7と同様にして型を準備する。
- バターは室温に戻しておく（指で押してみて軽くへこむ程度。やわらかくしすぎない。小さなさいころ状にしておくと早く室温に戻る）。
- 飾り用を除くピスタチオと粉糖をフードプロセッサーにかけて細かくし、アーモンドパウダーと一緒にふるっておく。
- 飾り用のピスタチオは好みの大きさに刻んでおく。
- オーブンを170℃に温める。

作り方

1. パート・ブリゼ・シュクレを作り、ピケ（多数）をして、から焼きする（p.48～50参照）。
2. グレープフルーツの果肉を取り出し、ざるに並べて水分をきる（果肉が分厚い場合は、$\frac{1}{2}$にそぎ切りにする）。
3. ピスタチオ＆プティ・ポワールのタルトの作り方（p.32）2、3を参照してクリームを作り、グランマルニエを加えてハンドミキサーでよくなじませる。直径1cmの丸口金をつけた絞出し袋に入れ、タルト台に絞って表面をスプーンで平らにし、グレープフルーツを並べて、オーブンで約1時間焼く。
4. 粗熱が取れたら、表面全体にグラサージュをはけでぬって、飾り用のピスタチオをまんべんなく散らし、型から出して網の上で冷ます。

食べごろ：1～3日目　冷やして

〈パート・ブリゼ・シュクレ生地を使って〉
クレーム&ブラックベリーのタルト
Tarte à la crème et aux mûres

わが家のデザートの定番「クレーム」を、タルトに入れて焼いてみました。クレームは、表面にカソナードをふりかけてバーナーで焼くと、クレーム・ブリュレになります。キャラメル、コーヒー、ジャスミンティー味。プレーンなものにベリー類をたっぷり入れるのも好きです。タルト台が湿りやすいので、その日のうちに食べきりましょう。

材料
（直径20cmのタルト型1台分）
パート・ブリゼ・シュクレ(p.48参照)　基本量
卵黄　38g
グラニュー糖　26g
生クリーム　85ml
牛乳　76ml
ブラックベリー（冷凍）　20個

準備
・p.7と同様にして型を準備する。
・ブラックベリーはペーパータオルの上で解凍しておく。
・オーブンを120℃に温める。

作り方
1 パート・ブリゼ・シュクレを作り、ピケをしないで、から焼きする（p.48～50参照。重しを取った後、ドレをしてさらに5分、もう一度ぬって5分焼く）。

2 ボウルに卵黄とグラニュー糖を入れて、グラニュー糖が溶けるまで泡立て器で混ぜる。

3 小鍋に生クリームと牛乳を入れ、鍋の縁が沸騰するまで温めて、**2**に注いで泡立て器でなじませる。

4 タルト台に**3**をこし器でこしながら入れ（表面の泡が気になるようなら、バーナーか「チャッカマン」で焼き飛ばす）、ブラックベリーを並べて、オーブンで約1時間焼き、粗熱が取れたら型ごと冷蔵庫で冷やす。

食べごろ：当日　冷やして

〈パート・ブリゼ・シュクレ生地を使って〉
タルト・オ・シトロン
Tarte au citron

ル・コルドン・ブルーに通っていたころ、学校の近くの惣菜店においしいタルト・オ・シトロンがあり、友人たちと毎日買いに行っていました。惣菜店、パン屋のものはレモンクリームをタルト台に詰めてから、さらに焼いていますが、パティスリーのものは焼かずに、メレンゲの代りに表面にグラサージュをかけるのが一般的です。

材料

(直径18×高さ2cmのタルトリング1台分)
パート・ブリゼ・シュクレ(p.48参照)　基本量
レモン汁　1/4カップ(約2個分)
全卵　95g
卵黄　40g
グラニュー糖　60g
レモンの皮のすりおろし　5g(約1個分)
バター　63g

イタリアン・メレンゲの材料

卵白　60g
グラニュー糖　40g
グラニュー糖(シロップ用)　50g
水　35ml

準備

- p.7と同様にして型を準備する。
- バターは8mm角に切って、使う直前まで冷蔵庫に入れておく。

作り方

1. パート・ブリゼ・シュクレを作り、タルトリングをクッキングシートの上にのせ、基本の作り方と同様にして生地を敷き込み、ピケ(表面のみ多数)をして、から焼きする(p.48〜50参照)。

2. 鍋にレモン汁を入れて、鍋の縁が沸騰するまで温める。全卵と卵黄をボウルに入れてときほぐし、グラニュー糖を加えて泡立て器で白っぽくなるまで混ぜる。

3. 卵のボウルにレモン汁を加え、泡立て器でなじませたら、混ぜ合わせた材料を鍋に戻し、レモンの皮のすりおろしを加えて、泡立て器で混ぜながら弱火で鍋底からポコッと沸騰するまで火を通す。

4. 3にバターを加えて、泡立て器でしっかりと混ぜ合わせ、バットに移して氷水に当てて粗熱を取る。クリームをタルト台に流し込み、スプーンで平らにする。

5. イタリアン・メレンゲを作る(p.51参照)。直径1cmの丸口金をつけた絞出し袋に入れて、メレンゲをつぼみのように絞り、側面をバーナーで焼き(バーナーがなければそのままで)、冷蔵庫で冷やす。

食べごろ：1〜2日目　冷やして

〈パート・ブリゼ・シュクレ生地を使って〉

チェリークラフティのタルト
Tarte de clafoutis aux cerises

耐熱容器にアパレイユを流し、チェリーをたっぷり入れて焼く、リムーザン地方のお菓子「クラフティ・リムーザン」をタルト台に流し込みました。洋梨、桃などでバリエーションが楽しめます。アパレイユの粉の量は家庭によって違い、かなり歯ごたえのあるものもありました（ひょっとして失敗？）。目分量で作っている人も多いようです。

材料
（直径20cmのタルト型1台分）
パート・ブリゼ・シュクレ（p.48参照）　基本量
全卵　60g
グラニュー糖　33g
塩　ひとつまみ
薄力粉　26g
ベーキングパウダー　1g（小さじ½）
牛乳　¼カップ
生クリーム　17ml
ラム酒　3ml
アメリカンダークチェリー（缶詰）　20個
粉糖（飾り用。お好みで）　適宜

準備
・p.7と同様にして型を準備する。
・粉類は合わせてふるっておく。
・チェリーは、ペーパータオルの上でしっかりと水分をきっておく。
・オーブンを170℃に温める。

作り方
1 パート・ブリゼ・シュクレを作り、ピケをしないで、から焼きする（p.48〜50参照）。

2 ボウルに全卵を入れて泡立て器でときほぐし、グラニュー糖と塩を加え、グラニュー糖と塩が溶けるまで混ぜる。粉類を加え、泡立て器で軽くなじませる。

3 小鍋に牛乳と生クリームを入れ、鍋の縁が沸騰するまで温め、2に注いで泡立て器で軽く混ぜたら、ラム酒を加えて泡立て器でなじませる。

4 タルト台に3をこし器でこしながら入れ、チェリーを並べて、オーブンで約40分焼き、粗熱が取れたら型ごと冷蔵庫で冷やし、お好みで粉糖をふる。

食べごろ：1〜2日目　粗熱を取って、冷やして

〈パート・ブリゼ・シュクレ生地を使って〉
ココナッツ&パイナップルのタルト
Tarte à la noix de coco râpée et aux ananas

パイナップル、パッションフルーツ、マンゴー、オレンジ+ココナッツ。このいかにも南国風な組合せが好きで、ムース、アイスクリーム、焼き菓子と、様々なお菓子に使っています。ココナッツは水分を吸収しやすいので、焼き菓子に使用するときは、卵、牛乳、リキュールなどの水分を多めに加えると、しっとりと仕上がります。

材料

（約25×10×高さ2.5cmのタルト型1台分）
パート・ブリゼ・シュクレ（p.48参照）　基本量
パイナップル　正味60g（小約1/4個）
バター　45g
グラニュー糖　45g
ココナッツファイン　25g
アーモンドパウダー　27g
全卵　50g
＊パイナップルは若くて、かためのものを使用。

バターは
小さなさいころ状に切っておくと、
早く室温に戻る。

準備

- p.7と同様にして型を準備する。
- バターは室温に戻しておく（指で押してみて軽くへこむ程度。やわらかくしすぎない）。
- 粉類は合わせてふるっておく。
- オーブンを170℃に温める。

作り方

1. パート・ブリゼ・シュクレを作り、ピケ（多数）をして、から焼きする（p.48〜50参照）。
2. パイナップルは縦1/4に切って、皮をむいて芯を取る。横5mm厚さに10枚スライスし、ざるに並べて水分をきる。
3. ボウルにバターとグラニュー糖を入れ、ハンドミキサーでバターがもったりとして白っぽくなるまで混ぜる。
4. 3に粉類を加え、ハンドミキサーで軽くなじませたら、全卵をよくときほぐして2〜3回に分けて加え（しっかりとなじんでから次を加える）、ハンドミキサーでよく混ぜる。
5. 4を直径1cmの丸口金をつけた絞出し袋に入れ、タルト台に絞って表面をスプーンで平らにし、パイナップルを並べて、オーブンで約55分焼き、粗熱が取れたら型から出して網の上で冷ます。

食べごろ：1〜2日目　冷やして

〈パート・ブリゼ・シュクレ生地を使って〉
ココア&プルーン&ナッツのタルト
Tarte à la poudre de cacao, aux pruneaux et aux noix

フランスの地方のショコラティエで出会った組合せ「ショコラ＋プルーン」。プルーンをショコラでコーティングしたお菓子で、絶品でしたので、「ココア＋プルーン」、彩りにピスタチオとくるみを加え、組合せを試してみたら正解でした！ ただちょっと見た目が地味ですが……。濃いめに入れたコーヒーとよく合います。

パート・ブリゼ・シュクレ・カカオの材料

（直径20cmのタルト型1台分）
薄力粉　115g
ココア　10g
グラニュー糖　30g
塩　1g
バター　75g
全卵　40g
水　4ml
＊薄力粉をふるいにかけ、ココアを目の細かい茶こしでふるい入れて、よく混ぜ合わせて使用する。

タルトの材料

アーモンドパウダー　48g
グラニュー糖　65g
全卵　80g
薄力粉　21g
ベーキングパウダー　1g（小さじ1/2）
ココア　16g
バター　30g
プルーン（セミドライ）　正味30g
くるみ　12g
くるみ（飾り用）　4個
ピスタチオ（皮なし・飾り用）　10g

準備

・p.7と同様にして型を準備する。
・アーモンドパウダーはふるっておく。
・薄力粉、ベーキングパウダーは合わせてふるい、ココアを目の細かい茶こしでふるい入れて、よく混ぜ合わせておく。
・オーブンを180℃に温める。

作り方

1 パート・ブリゼ・シュクレ・カカオを作り、ピケ（多数）をして、から焼きする（p.48〜50参照）。プルーンは種を取って好みの大きさに切る。くるみは飾り用ともに1/4に切る。

2 ボウルにアーモンドパウダー、グラニュー糖を入れ、全卵を加えて、泡立て器で白っぽくなるまで混ぜる。

3 2に粉類を加え、ゴムべらですくい上げるようにして粉類が見えなくなるまで混ぜ、とかしバターをゴムべらに伝わせながら加えて、バターが見えなくなるまで混ぜたら、プルーンとくるみを加えて軽く混ぜる。

4 タルト台に3を流し、飾り用のくるみとピスタチオをのせて、オーブンで約25分焼き、粗熱が取れたら型から出して網の上で冷ます。

食べごろ：2〜3日目　冷やして

〈パート・ブリゼ・シュクレ生地を使って〉
抹茶&茶福豆のタルト
Tarte au thé vert et aux chafukumamés

和菓子好きが高じて、和素材を使ったフランス菓子をおやつによく作ります。特に、抹茶をふんだんに使った濃厚なものが好きで、ちょっと贅沢ですが味わい豊かな「丸久小山園」のものを常備しています。中の生地がしっとり、もっちりとした食感のこのタルトは、茶福豆との相性が抜群。おいしい緑茶とともにいただきましょう。

材料
（直径20cmのタルト型1台分）
パート・ブリゼ・シュクレ(p.48参照)　基本量
アーモンドパウダー　50g
グラニュー糖　70g
全卵　88g
薄力粉　35g
ベーキングパウダー　1g(小さじ½)
抹茶　4.5g(大さじ1)
バター　30g
茶福豆　18個
＊「ふじっこ」の茶福豆を使用。

準備
- p.7と同様にして型を準備する。
- アーモンドパウダーはふるっておく。
- 薄力粉、ベーキングパウダーは合わせてふるい、抹茶を目の細かい茶こしでふるい入れて、よく混ぜ合わせておく。
- オーブンを180℃に温める。

作り方
1 パート・ブリゼ・シュクレを作り、ピケ(多数)をして、から焼きする（p.48～50参照）。

2 ボウルにアーモンドパウダー、グラニュー糖を入れ、全卵を加えて、泡立て器で白っぽくなるまで混ぜる。

3 2に粉類を加え、ゴムべらですくい上げるようにして粉類が見えなくなるまで混ぜ、とかしバターをゴムべらに伝わせながら加えて、バターが見えなくなるまで混ぜる。

4 タルト台に茶福豆を並べ（飾り用に3個残す）、3を流して（表面をならさずに焼くと、焼上りの表情がかわいい）茶福豆をのせて、オーブンで約35分焼き、粗熱が取れたら型から出して網の上で冷ます。

食べごろ：2～3日目　常温、冷やして

「丸久小山園」の抹茶は味わい深く、お菓子の仕上りが違います。
Tel. 0774-20-0909

パート・ブリゼ（シュクレ、サレ）
Pâte brisée (sucrée, salée)

甘味の「シュクレ」、塩味の「サレ」。どちらも作り方は同じで、パイに似たサクサクとした食感が特徴です。フードプロセッサーで作る方法もありますが、手で作るとバターの粒の大きさにばらつきが出て、焼成後、それが食感に変化を生み、味に奥行きが出ますので、こちらの方法をおすすめします。成功の秘訣は、バターをとかさないこと。

パート・ブリゼ・シュクレの材料

（基本量・約25×10×2.5cmのタルト型1台分）
薄力粉　115g
グラニュー糖　25g
塩　1g
バター　60g
全卵　32g
水　3ml
強力粉（打ち粉用）2種共通　適宜
全卵（ドレ用）2種共通　適宜

パート・ブリゼ・サレの材料

（基本量・約25×10×2.5cmのタルト型1台分）
薄力粉　115g
塩　2g
バター　60g
全卵　35g
水　5ml

準備

- バターは8mm角に切って、使用するまで冷蔵庫に入れておく。
- 全卵をよくときほぐし、水と合わせておく。
- クッキングシートを型より一回り大きく切っておく。
- p.7と同様にして型を準備する。
- オーブンを180℃に温める。

作り方（2種共通）

ボウルに薄力粉をふるいながら入れ、グラニュー糖（シュクレのみ）、塩を加えて、泡立て器で材料がまんべんなく混ざるまで混ぜ、バターを加えてカードでざっと刻んだら、指先でバターをつぶす。

2 1の中央にくぼみを作り、そこに合わせておいた全卵と水を加えて、ボウルをときどき回しながらカードをボウルの中で前後させ、生地全体を軽くなじませる(生地は粉っぽい状態。室温が高いときは、冷蔵庫で冷やす)。

3 2を両手でギュッと握って台の上に重ねて置き、手のひらの腹で、生地を台にすりつけながら向う側に移動させる。ひととおり移動したら、カードで生地をひとまとめにし、ラップで包んで平らにして、冷蔵庫で1時間から一晩休ませる。

4 生地を2回折りたたみ、手のひらでギュッと押さえ、なじんだら球状に丸める。台とめん棒に打ち粉をふり、めん棒を軽く動かしながら、生地が4mm厚さになるまで少しずつのばす。

5 生地に型を当て、大きさ(底面+高さ+α)が充分かどうかを確認したら、生地についた打ち粉をはけで払い、生地を型の上にふんわりとのせる。生地の端を両手で持ち、下に向かって押し込むようにしながら一周し、型からはみ出た部分を外に向かって折る。型の上にめん棒を転がして、余分な生地を切り落とす。

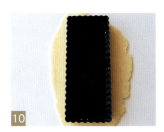

6 親指と人さし指で側面を挟みながら一周する。残り生地を丸めて四隅を押さえ、生地を型に密着させる。フォークで生地の底面にピケし、冷蔵庫で20分休ませる。

7 **6**の上にクッキングシートを敷き込み、重しを入れる。シートをしっかりと側面に沿わせ（四隅は生地に合わせてタックをとる）、縁のほうが多くなるように重しを調節する。

8 あらかじめ熱しておいたオーブンで20分焼き、重しを取ってドレをして、さらに約10分焼き、型に入れたまま網の上で充分に冷ます。

＊この生地は水を加えるため傷みやすく、保存は冷蔵庫で約2日、冷凍庫で約1か月。まとめて作って密封し、すぐに冷凍しておくと便利。解凍は室温または冷蔵庫で。

イタリアン・メレンゲ
Meringue italienne

材料
卵白 60g
グラニュー糖 40g
グラニュー糖（シロップ用） 50g
水 35ml

作り方

1. ボウルに卵白を入れて、ハンドミキサーでしっかりと泡立てたら、グラニュー糖を2回に分けて加え、ハンドミキサーを持ち上げたときに、ふんわりと優しい角が立つまで泡立てる（泡立てすぎると絞りにくい）。

2. 小鍋にシロップ用のグラニュー糖、水を入れて火にかける（鍋の側面に飛び散ったシロップは、焦げるもととなるので、水でぬらしたはけでふき取る）。沸騰してプティ・ブレ（117℃）になるまで煮つめたら、1のボウルに少しずつ加えながらハンドミキサー（高速）で、ふんわりと優しい角が立つまで泡立てる。

＊沸騰したシロップに少しとろみがついてきたら、スプーンですくって水の中に入れ、手に取ってやわらかいボール状にまとめることができる状態がプティ・ブレ。

タルト・オ・シトロン（p.38）の メレンゲの絞り方

絞出し袋をよくねじって、袋がしっかりと張った状態にし、レモンクリームの上に押しつけるような感覚で、メレンゲを勢いよく絞り出し、ゆっくりと絞出し袋を真上に引く。

Pâte brisée salée

Part 3
前菜やメインに
Pour entrée et plat principal

前菜やメインに最適な塩味のタルト「キッシュ」。
アパレイユに入れる塩分は、具材やフロマージュの塩気によって違ってきますので、
お好みの味に調節してください。
一度で食べきれずに冷めてしまったら、アルミフォイルで包んで、
オーブンまたはオーブントースターで温め直しましょう。

〈パート・ブリゼ・サレ生地を使って〉
グリーンアスパラガス&
スモークサーモンのキッシュ
Quiche au saumon fumé et aux asperges vertes

フロマージュ。以前は、高級スーパーや専門店に買いに行っていましたが、近ごろは近所のスーパーでも、多種多様なものがそろうようになりました。私も普段は手近なシュレッドタイプのものを使っていますが、特別な日にはちょっぴり贅沢をして、グリュイエール、エメンタール、コンテ、ラクレットなどをすりおろして使っています。

材料

（直径20cmのタルト型1台分）
パート・ブリゼ・サレ(p.48参照)　基本量
全卵　57g
卵黄　17g
生クリーム　96ml
塩、こしょう、ナツメッグ　各適宜
グリーンアスパラガス　5本
スモークサーモン　10枚(約90g)
チーズ(シュレッドタイプ)　50g
ケイパー　6g
ディル(飾り用)　適宜
＊ケイパーは、ペーパータオルの上で水分をきってから計量する。

準備

- p.7と同様にして型を準備する。
- チーズは粗みじんの大きさに刻んでおく。
- オーブンを180℃に温める。

作り方

1. パート・ブリゼ・サレを作り、ピケ（表面のみ多数）をして、から焼きする（p.48〜50参照）。
2. アスパラガスは型の長さに合わせて切り、塩を入れた湯でかためにゆでて氷水にとり、ペーパータオルで水分をよくふき取って、スモークサーモンを巻きつける。
3. タルト台に1/2量のチーズをまんべんなく散らし、2を並べて、間にケイパーを散らす。
4. ボウルに全卵、卵黄、生クリーム、塩、こしょう、ナツメッグを入れて泡立て器でよく混ぜ合わせ、3にこし器でこしながら入れ、残りのチーズをまんべんなく散らして、オーブンで約35分焼き、ディルを添えていただく。

食べごろ：当日　焼きたて

塩気と香りがやさしい「よつ葉乳業」のシュレッドチーズ。
Tel.0120-428-841

〈パート・ブリゼ・サレ生地を使って〉
きのこのキッシュ
Quiche aux champignons japonais

フランスでは、秋から初冬にかけてジロール、セープなどのきのこが八百屋の店先に並び、この時期必ず作りたくなるのが「きのこのキッシュ」。その日本バージョンをご紹介しましょう。きのこは種類によって水分の出方が違うので、種類ごとにていねいに炒めるのがコツです。ベルギー・エシャロットを刻んで入れても美味。

材料
（直径20cmのタルト型1台分）
パート・ブリゼ・サレ(p.48参照)　基本量
全卵　40g
卵黄　13g
生クリーム　97ml
しいたけ　正味45g
エリンギ　正味50g
しめじ　正味80g
サラダオイル、塩、こしょう　各適宜
チャービル(飾り用)　適宜
＊しいたけは軸を取った分量。

準備
- p.7と同様にして型を準備する。
- オーブンを180℃に温める。

作り方
1 パート・ブリゼ・サレを作り、ピケ（表面のみ多数）をして、から焼きする（p.48〜50参照）。

2 しいたけは½に切って3mm厚さにスライス。エリンギは石づきを取り、4cm長さに切って縦3mm厚さにスライス。しめじは石づきを取ってほぐす。

3 フライパンにサラダオイルを入れて**2**を種類ごとに軽く炒め、強めに塩、こしょうをする。ざるに入れて余分な水分をきり、タルト台に入れる。

4 ボウルに全卵、卵黄、生クリーム、塩、こしょうを入れて泡立て器でよく混ぜ合わせ、**3**にこし器でこしながら入れ、チャービルをのせて、オーブンで約35分焼く。

食べごろ：当日　焼きたて

〈パート・ブリゼ・サレ生地を使って〉

キッシュ・ロレーヌ
Quiche lorraine

ロレーヌ地方の名物キッシュ。フランス人は、キッシュを前菜にすることが多く、その後メイン、デザートと進んでいくのですが、かわいい胃袋？の日本人は、サラダを添えるだけで充分メインになります。ロレーヌ地方に行くと、カフェ、レストラン、至る所でお目にかかりますが、どこのものも特大サイズ。恐るべし、フランス人の胃袋！

材料

（直径20cmのタルト型1台分）
パート・ブリゼ・サレ(p.48参照)　基本量
全卵　70g
卵黄　20g
生クリーム　115ml
塩、こしょう、ナツメッグ　各適宜
ベーコン　100g
チーズ（シュレッドタイプ）　50g
サラダオイル　適宜
＊ベーコンは塊のものを使用するとより本格的だが、なければスライスで。

準備

- p.7と同様にして型を準備する。
- チーズは粗みじんの大きさに刻んでおく。
- オーブンを180℃に温める。

作り方

1. パート・ブリゼ・サレを作り、ピケ（表面のみ多数）をして、から焼きする（p.48～50参照）。

2. ベーコンは7mm厚さにスライスし、さらに7mm幅の棒状に切る。フライパンにサラダオイルを入れてベーコンを軽く炒め、強めにこしょうをし、ペーパータオルの上で余分な脂分を取ってタルト台に入れ、1/2量のチーズを散らす。

3. ボウルに全卵、卵黄、生クリーム、塩、こしょう、ナツメッグを入れて泡立て器でよく混ぜ合わせ、2にこし器でこしながら入れ、残りのチーズをまんべんなく散らして、オーブンで約30分焼く。

食べごろ：当日　焼きたて

パート・ブリゼ・サレは底がふくれやすいので、焼き上がったらすぐに、上からやさしく押さえる。

そら豆&グリーンピースのキッシュ+にんじんサラダ
Quiche aux fèves et petits pois accompagnée d'une salade de carottes

チーズフォンデュのタルト
Tarte au fromage fondu

〈パート・ブリゼ・サレ生地を使って〉
そら豆 & グリーンピースのキッシュ
＋
にんじんサラダ

Quiche aux fèves et petits pois accompagnée d'une salade de carottes

フランスにもそら豆、グリーンピースがあり、価格も手ごろなのでたっぷりと使うことができ、日本を懐かしんで豆ご飯、ひすい煮、うぐいすあんなど、よく作りました。キッシュのアパレイユは、全卵を使うのが一般的ですが、具材から出る水分を受け止めるとともに、こくが増す、卵黄を加えるのが私流です。ぜひお試しください。

材料

（直径20cmのタルト型1台分）
パート・ブリゼ・サレ（p.48参照）　基本量
全卵　45g
卵黄　15g
生クリーム　110ml
そら豆　正味60g
グリーンピース　正味70g
ベーコン（スライス）　50g
チーズ（シュレッドタイプ）　50g
サラダオイル、塩、こしょう　各適宜

にんじんサラダの材料

にんじん　適宜
チャービル（飾り用）　適宜
ドレッシング　適宜

準備

- p.7と同様にして型を準備する。
- チーズは粗みじんの大きさに刻んでおく。
- オーブンを180℃に温める。

作り方

1 パート・ブリゼ・サレを作り、ピケ（表面のみ多数）をして、から焼きする（p.48～50参照）。

2 そら豆とグリーンピースは、塩を入れた湯でかためにゆでてざるに上げ、自然に冷ます（そら豆の薄皮が気になるようなら取り除いてもいい）。

3 ベーコンは5mm幅に切り、フライパンにサラダオイルを入れて軽く色づくまで炒め、強めにこしょうをして、ペーパータオルの上で余分な脂分を取る。タルト台に½量のチーズを散らし、ベーコン、2の順番に重ねる。

4 ボウルに全卵、卵黄、生クリーム、塩、こしょうを入れて泡立て器でよく混ぜ合わせ、3にこし器でこしながら入れ、残りのチーズをまんべんなく散らして、オーブンで約30分焼く。にんじんをチーズおろし器でおろし（なければせん切り）、チャービルを添えて、お好みのドレッシングでいただく。

食べごろ：当日　焼きたて

〈パート・ブリゼ・サレ生地を使って〉
チーズフォンデュのタルト
Tarte au fromage fondu

チーズフォンデュは溶かしたチーズにパンや野菜をつけていただきますが、これは逆バージョン。いつもは耐熱容器に直接入れますが、今回はタルト仕立てにしてみました。パンのつけ込みとタルトのから焼きを前日にしておくと、翌日は合わせて焼くだけ。週末のブランチにぴったりです。生ハム、ピクルス、ワインとともに召し上がれ。

材料
（24×16×高さ7cmの耐熱容器1台分）
パート・ブリゼ・サレ(p.48参照)　基本量の1.5倍
フランスパン　50g
水　85ml
白ワイン(辛口)　40ml
チーズ　60g
塩、こしょう　各適宜
ブロッコリー　正味65g
＊チーズはエメンタール、グリュイエール、ラクレットなどがおすすめ。

準備
・p.7と同様にして型を準備する。
・チーズはすりおろす。
・オーブンを180℃に温める。

作り方

1 フランスパンを3cm角に切り、縁の深いお皿に入れる。

2 小鍋に水と白ワインを入れ、沸騰したら火から下ろす。チーズを加えて、泡立て器でよく混ぜて溶かし、塩、こしょうで味を調え、1の上にかけて、粗熱を取って冷蔵庫で一晩おく。

3 パート・ブリゼ・サレを作り、ピケ（多数）をして、から焼きする（p.48〜50参照。180℃で30分焼き、重しを取ってドレをして、さらに約15分焼く）。

4 ブロッコリーは小房に分け、塩を入れた湯でかためにゆでて氷水にとり、ペーパータオルで水分をよくふき取る。

5 タルト台に2とブロッコリー（つぼみが開いている場合は焦げるので、焼き上がる3分前に加える）を入れ、オーブンで約30分焼く。

食べごろ：当日　焼きたて

炒め玉ねぎ&じゃがいも&カマンベールのタルト
Tarte à l'oignon, aux pommes de terre et au camembert

南仏野菜のキッシュ
Quiche aux légumes du Midi

〈パート・ブリゼ・サレ生地を使って〉
炒め玉ねぎ&じゃがいも&カマンベールのタルト

Tarte à l'oignon, aux pommes de terre et au camembert

サヴォワ地方の家庭料理「タルティフレット」は、炒め玉ねぎ、じゃがいも、ベーコンを耐熱容器に重ねて入れ、この地方のフロマージュ「ルブロション」を、丸ごと中央にのせてオーブンで焼く、ワイルドな料理。それをタルトの中に入れ、入手しやすいカマンベールに置き換えてみました。カマンベールの熟成ぐあいはお好みで。

材料
(直径20cmのタルト型1台分)
パート・ブリゼ・サレ(p.48参照)　基本量の1.5倍
玉ねぎ　大1個(約150g)
サラダオイル、塩、こしょう　各適宜
じゃがいも(メークイン)　大1個(約160g)
カマンベール　70g

準備
・p.7と同様にして型を準備する。
・オーブンを180℃に温める。

作り方
1. パート・ブリゼ・サレを作って4mm厚さにのばし、直径24cmに切って型より少し高くラフに敷き込み、ピケ(表面のみ多数)をして、から焼きする(p.48〜50参照)。
2. 鍋にサラダオイルを入れ、½に切って繊維に直角にスライスした玉ねぎを、薄いきつね色になるまで炒め(焦げそうになったら、少量の水を加える)、仕上げに塩、こしょうをする。
3. じゃがいもは皮のまま、塩を入れて水から竹串がすっと通るまでゆで、皮をむいて8mm厚さの輪切りにする。カマンベールは好みの大きさに切る。
4. タルト台にじゃがいもを並べ、こしょうをする。炒め玉ねぎをまんべんなく広げ、カマンベールをのせてこしょうをし、オーブンで約30分焼く。

食べごろ：当日　焼きたて

〈パート・ブリゼ・サレ生地を使って〉
南仏野菜のキッシュ
Quiche aux légumes du Midi

ズッキーニ、なす、トマト。フランスのタルト専門店やサロン・ドゥ・テでよく見る組合せ。とびきり甘いフルーツトマトを使うと、味が引き立ちます。ズッキーニとなすをさいころ状に切ってオリーヴオイルで炒め、エルブ・ドゥ・プロヴァンスをたっぷりかけたものを、アパレイユの中に入れて焼くのも南仏っぽくておすすめです。

材料
(約25×10×高さ2.5cmのタルト型1台分)
パート・ブリゼ・サレ(p.48参照)　基本量
全卵　35g
卵黄　12g
生クリーム　85ml
塩、こしょう　各適宜
フルーツトマト　約1個
ズッキーニ　約1/4本
なす　約1/3本
チーズ(シュレッドタイプ)　50g
タイム(飾り用)　適宜

準備
・p.7と同様にして型を準備する。
・チーズは粗みじんの大きさに刻んでおく。
・オーブンを180℃に温める。

作り方
1. パート・ブリゼ・サレを作り、ピケ(表面のみ多数)をして、から焼きする(p.48～50参照)。
2. トマトは5mm厚さ、ズッキーニ、なすは7mm厚さの輪切りにし(各6枚)、なすは水につけてあくを抜き、ペーパータオルで水分を取る。
3. タルト台に1/2量のチーズを散らし、ズッキーニ、トマト、なすの順番に2列に並べ、塩、こしょうをする。
4. ボウルに全卵、卵黄、生クリーム、塩、こしょうを入れて泡立て器でよく混ぜ合わせ、3にこし器でこしながら入れ、残りのチーズ、タイムをまんべんなく散らして、オーブンで約40分焼く。

食べごろ：当日　焼きたて

微量でも味に違いが出る塩、抹茶、ふくらみに影響するベーキングパウダーなどをはかるのに便利なスケール。

Part 4
2番生地を使ってアレンジ
Préparer autrement les pâtes restantes

抹茶のミルフイユ
Mille-feuille au thé vert

残った生地を保存しておけば、立派なデザートやおつまみに変身します。
残り生地は、打ち粉をはけでよく払い、随時ラップをして冷凍し、
使うときは室温または冷蔵庫で解凍しましょう。

シュクレ&黒ごま+抹茶アイス
Sésame noir+thé vert

シュクレ+紫いもアイス
Normale+patate douce violette

シュクレ&紅茶の葉+紅茶アイス
Thé+thé

シュクレ・カカオ+ショコラアイス
Cacao+chocolat

抹茶のミルフイユ
Mille-feuille au thé vert

渡仏当初、抹茶のお菓子が食べたくて、抹茶色のものを見かけるとつい買ってしまい、食べてみると「ピスタチオ」でがっかりしたものです。でも、最近ではフランスでも抹茶が普及し、ピスタチオと思って買ったら……なんてことも。このケーキは、タルト生地のサクサク感を楽しみたいので、供する直前に組み立てましょう。

材料
（4個分）
パート・ブリゼ・シュクレ　約350g
抹茶のクレーム・パティシエール
卵黄　30g
グラニュー糖　45g
薄力粉　5g
コーンスターチ　5g
抹茶　3g
牛乳　158ml

準備
・天板にクッキングシートを敷いておく。
・オーブンを180℃に温める。
・薄力粉、コーンスターチは合わせてふるい、抹茶を目の細かい茶こしでふるい入れて、よく混ぜ合わせておく。

作り方

1 パート・ブリゼ・シュクレを5mm厚さにのばし、ピケ（多数）をして、4×9cmを12枚切り、冷蔵庫で20分休ませた後、網をのせて20分焼き、網を取ってドレをして、さらに約10分オーブンで焼く。

2 ボウルに卵黄とグラニュー糖を入れて、泡立て器で白くもったりとするまですり混ぜ、粉類を加えて、泡立て器でよくなじませる。

3 鍋に牛乳を入れて火にかけ、鍋の縁が沸騰してきたら、2のボウルに少量加えて泡立て器でなじませ、残りを加え、泡立て器でよく混ぜて、こし器でこしながら鍋に戻す。

4 3を火にかけ、泡立て器で勢いよく混ぜながら、クリーム状になって、鍋底からふつふつと沸騰して、粘り気がなくなるまで火を通し、バットに移して、ラップをぴったりとかぶせ、氷水をバットの底に当てて、粗熱を取る。

5 4を泡立て器で混ぜて、直径1cmの口金をつけた絞出し袋に入れ、1の1枚の上に角のように2列絞り出し、もう1枚のせて同様に絞り出し、さらにもう1枚のせる。

シュクレ&黒ごま+抹茶アイス
Sésame noir + thé vert

シュクレ+紫いもアイス
Normale + patate douce violette

シュクレ&紅茶の葉+紅茶アイス
Thé + thé

シュクレ・カカオ+ショコラアイス
Cacao + chocolat

著書『アイスクリーム大好き！』は、当時住んでいたパリのアパルトマンで撮影しましたが、真冬の寒い最中、アパルトマンは全館暖房で調節ができず、窓を全開して背中にカイロをはり、とけるアイスとの戦いでした。今回ご紹介するのは、スペースの関係上4種類ですが、組合せは自由自在。お好きな組合せを見つけてください。

材料
(各3〜5人分)
パート・シュクレ（カカオ）　各約100g
黒ごま　2g
紅茶　2g
アイスクリーム　適宜
＊黒ごま、紅茶はパート100gに対する分量

準備
・天板にクッキングシートを敷いておく。
・オーブンを180℃に温める。

作り方
1. 黒ごま、紅茶はそれぞれ生地にまぶし、軽く練り込む。パート・シュクレ（カカオ）を好みの厚さ（3〜5mm）にのばし、ピケをしないで、直径8cmの菊型で抜き、冷蔵庫で20分休ませた後、網をのせて20分焼き、網を取ってドレをして、さらに約10分オーブンで焼く。
2. アイスクリームをのせていただく。

フリュイ・ルージュ+クレーム・パティシエール
Fruits rouges+crème pâtissière

マスカルポーネ+マンゴー+はちみつ
Mascarpone+mangue+miel

フォレ・ノワール
Forêt-noire

フリュイ・ルージュ
＋
クレーム・パティシエール
Fruits rouges + crème pâtissière

日本で売られている冷凍ラズベリーは、フランスで売られているものに比べ、種が大きくてかたく、裏ごしにかけないといただきにくいので、本当に残念。このデザートは、さわやかな酸味のラズベリーソースと、極限まで粉の量を減らした、とろーりとろけるカスタードクリームの組合せ。生のベリーをたっぷりとのせて召し上がれ。

材料
(4人分)
パート・ブリゼ・シュクレ　約200g
お好みのベリー　適宜
ミント(飾り用)　適宜

クレーム・パティシエールの材料
卵黄　40g
グラニュー糖　44g
薄力粉　4g
コーンスターチ　2g
牛乳　1カップ

ラズベリーソースの材料
(作りやすい分量)
ラズベリー(冷凍)　100g
グラニュー糖　35g
レモン汁　大さじ1
＊冷凍ラズベリーは
ペーパータオルの上でとかしてから計量する。

ラズベリーソースの作り方
すべての材料を鍋に入れ、ラズベリーから水分が出るまで2〜3時間おいて火にかけ、あくを取りながら軽くとろみがつくまで煮つめ、熱いうちにざるでこして種を取り除く。

準備
・天板にクッキングシートを敷いておく。
・オーブンを180℃に温める。

作り方
1　パート・ブリゼ・シュクレを5mm厚さにのばし、ピケ(多数)をして、直径10cmの菊型で4枚抜き、冷蔵庫で20分休ませた後、網をのせて20分焼き、網を取ってドレをして、さらに約10分オーブンで焼く。

2　抹茶のミルフイユの作り方(p.70) **2〜4**を参照してクリームを作り、冷蔵庫で冷やしておく。

3　皿にソースを絞り出し、**1**を中央に置いてベリーをのせ、**2**を泡立て器で混ぜて上からかけ、ミントを飾ってさらにベリーを散らす。

マスカルポーネといえば、『アイスクリーム大好き！』でご紹介した「ティラミスアイス」。わがレシピながら、あれは絶品です。機会があれば、作ってみてください。今回ご紹介するグラスデザートは、生クリームやマスカルポーネが中途半端に残ったとき、常備している材料でささっとできて、おいしい優れもの。こちらもぜひお試しください。

マスカルポーネ＋マンゴー＋はちみつ
Mascarpone＋mangue＋miel

材料

（グラス2個分）
パート・ブリゼ・シュクレ　約55g
マスカルポーネ　140g
グラニュー糖　9g
牛乳　8ml
マンゴー（冷凍）　6切れ
はちみつ　4g
ミント（飾り用）　適宜

準備（2種共通）

・天板にクッキングシートを敷いておく。
・オーブンを180℃に温める。

作り方

1. パート・ブリゼ・シュクレ（カカオ）を4mm厚さにのばし、ピケをしないで、冷蔵庫で20分休ませた後、オーブンで約30分焼く（2種共通）。
2. ボウルにマスカルポーネ、グラニュー糖、牛乳を入れて泡立て器でよく混ぜ合わせる。
3. グラスに½量の2を入れて、1を好みの大きさに砕いて入れ、残りの2を入れてマンゴーをのせ、はちみつをかけてミントを飾る。

フォレ・ノワール
Forêt-noire

材料

（グラス2個分）
パート・ブリゼ・シュクレ・カカオ　約55g
生クリーム　½カップ
グラニュー糖　20g
グリオッティーヌ　10個
チョコレート　適宜
＊グリオッティーヌは、
小粒のさくらんぼのリキュール漬け。

作り方

1. ボウルに生クリームとグラニュー糖を入れ、ボウルの底を氷水に当てて、泡立て器で6～7分に泡立てる。
2. グラスに½量の1を入れて、焼いたタルトを好みの大きさに砕いて入れ（飾り用を残す）、グリオッティーヌを入れて（飾り用2個を残す）、残りの1を入れ、飾り用のタルトとグリオッティーヌをのせて、削ったチョコレートを散らす。

ブリゼ・サレ・スティック
（プレーン、黒ごま、パルメザン）
Bâtons de pâte brisée salée (nature, au sésame noir et au fromage)

タラマ
Tarama

ディップ
Dip

Kiri + チャイブ & チャービル　　Kiri + herbes

Kiri + フルーツトマト　　Kiri + tomate

Kiri + アヴォカド　　Kiri + avocat

Kiri + サルタナレーズン　　Kiri + raisins de sultane

ブリゼ・サレ・スティック
（プレーン、黒ごま、パルメザン）
Bâtons de pâte brisée salée
(nature, au sésame noir et au fromage)

フランスのスーパー、惣菜店で必ず見かける「タラマ」。でも、手作りしようとたらこを探しても、どこにも見当たらず……。結局あきらめて、惣菜店で買っていました。カリカリに焼いたセーグルパンやブリニにのせて食べるのもいいですが、ブリゼ・サレ・スティックのプレーン、黒ごまとの相性も抜群。白ワインのお供にどうぞ。

タラマ
Tarama

材料

パート・ブリゼ・サレ　適宜
全卵（ドレ用）　適宜
黒ごま、パルメザンチーズ　各適宜

準備

・天板にクッキングシートを敷いておく。
・オーブンを180℃に温める。

作り方

パート・ブリゼ・サレを4mm厚さにのばし、ピケ（多数）をして、1.5×10cmの棒状に切り、冷蔵庫で20分休ませる。ドレをして（プレーンはしない）、黒ごま、パルメザンチーズを表面にまぶし、オーブンで約30分焼く。

材料

（作りやすい分量）
じゃがいも（メークイン）　140g（中約1個）
たらこ（生食用）　正味40g（約½腹）
生クリーム　大さじ1
レモン汁　小さじ½強
塩、こしょう　各適宜

作り方

1 じゃがいもは皮のまま、塩を入れて水から竹串がすっと通るまでゆで、熱いうちに皮をむいてマッシャーかすりこぎでつぶし、粗熱を取る。

2 たらこは皮の中身をスプーンで取り出し、1、生クリーム、レモン汁を加えてよく混ぜ合わせ、塩、こしょうで味を調える。

ディップ
Dip

フランスのクリームチーズ「Kiri」を使って作る、簡単ディップ。アペリティフのお供に最適です。フランスでは、夕食前のアペリティフに招かれることも多く、その場合は夕食が出ず、シャンパンと高級惣菜店の一口サイズの前菜＋おしゃべりが一般的でした。ただ、渡仏当初は、おいとまするタイミングがわからず、失敗も数知れず……。

Kiri＋チャイブ＆チャービル
Kiri＋herbes

材料
（2人分）
Kiri（クリームチーズ）　40g
チャイブ、チャービル　各適宜

作り方
Kiriを小さな器に入れ、スプーンでやわらかくなるまで練って、チャイブとチャービルをキッチンばさみで切りながら加え、スプーンで混ぜ合わせる。

Kiri＋フルーツトマト
Kiri＋tomate

材料
（2人分）
Kiri　40g
フルーツトマト　正味10g
こしょう　適宜

作り方
Kiriを小さな器に入れ、スプーンでやわらかくなるまで練って、皮のまま8mm角に切ったトマトを種つきのまま加え、こしょうをしてスプーンで混ぜ合わせる。

Kiri＋アヴォカド
Kiri＋avocat

材料
（2人分）
Kiri　40g
アヴォカド　正味40g（約1/2個）
塩、こしょう　各適宜

作り方
アヴォカドは1/2に切って種を取り、スプーンですくって小さな器に入れて、フォークでつぶす。別の器にKiriを入れ、スプーンでやわらかくなるまで練って、アヴォカド、塩、こしょうを加え、スプーンで混ぜ合わせる。

Kiri＋サルタナレーズン
Kiri＋raisins de sultane

材料
（2人分）
Kiri　40g
サルタナレーズン　10g

作り方
Kiriを小さな器に入れ、スプーンでやわらかくなるまで練って、好みの大きさに刻んだレーズンを加え、スプーンで混ぜ合わせる。

スモークサーモンのサラダ + バルサミコドレッシング
Salade de saumon fumé accompagnée d'une vinaigrette au vinaigre balsamique

完熟トマトのピッツァ
Pizza aux tomates

サーモンのリエット
Rillettes de saumon

アヴォカド+えび
Avocat+crevettes

スモークサーモンのサラダ＋バルサミコドレッシング
Salade de saumon fumé accompagnée d'une vinaigrette au vinaigre balsamique

このサラダは、来客のときの前菜によく作ります。今回はパート・ブリゼを使いましたが、折りパイを使ったり、キャビアをのせるとさらに豪華に。教室のベランダには、クラスで使うハーブを栽培しているので、とりたてをサラダにたっぷりと入れて、楽しんでいます。飾りのピーマンは、指先ではじき飛ばすときれいに散らばります。

材料

（4人分）
パート・ブリゼ・サレ　約250g
スモークサーモン　12枚
ベビーリーフ、ディル　各適宜
ピーマン、赤パプリカ、チャービル、
　ナスタチューム（飾り用）　各適宜

バルサミコドレッシングの材料

バルサミコ酢　小さじ2
赤ワインヴィネガー　小さじ2
粒マスタード　小さじ1/2
グラニュー糖　小さじ1/2強
塩　1g
こしょう　適宜
オリーヴオイル　大さじ1

準備

・天板にクッキングシートを敷いておく。
・オーブンを180℃に温める。

作り方

1. パート・ブリゼ・サレを5mm厚さにのばし、ピケ（多数）をして、直径10cmの菊型で4枚抜き、冷蔵庫で20分休ませた後、網をのせて20分焼き、網を取ってドレをして、さらに約10分オーブンで焼く。

2. ボウルにオリーヴオイル以外のドレッシングの材料を入れ、グラニュー糖、塩が溶けるまで泡立て器で混ぜる。そこにオリーヴオイルを加えながら、泡立て器でよく混ぜる。ピーマン、赤パプリカは、2mm角に切る。

3. 皿の中央に1を置き、サーモン、ベビーリーフとディルをドレッシングであえたもの、ナスタチュームの順にのせ、ピーマン、赤パプリカを皿に散らして、ドレッシングをかけ、チャービルを飾る。

2種類のサーモンが楽しめる、ライムの酸味がさわやかな「サーモンのリエット」。周知の組合せ「アヴォカドとえび」。ダイナミックな「完熟トマトのピッツァ」。いずれも前菜にぴったりの一品。トマトのピッツァは玉ねぎをしっかりと炒め、糖度の高いフルーツトマトを使うのがポイント。

完熟トマトのピッツァ
Pizza aux tomates

材料(3〜4人分)

パート・ブリゼ・サレ　200g	サラダオイル、塩、
玉ねぎ　中1個	こしょう　各適宜
フルーツトマト　1個	タイム(飾り用)　適宜
ベーコン(スライス)　40g	

作り方

1 パート・ブリゼ・サレを5mm厚さにラフにのばし、ピケ(多数)をして、冷蔵庫で20分休ませた後、オーブンで20分焼き、ドレをしてさらに約10分焼く。玉ねぎを炒める(p.66参照)。ベーコンは1/2に切る。トマトは5mm厚さの輪切りにする。

2 タルト台に炒め玉ねぎを広げ、ベーコンをのせてこしょうをする。トマトをのせて塩、こしょうをし、タイムを散らして、オーブンで約25分焼く。

サーモンのリエット
Rillettes de saumon

材料(6個分)

パート・ブリゼ・サレ　約150g
ライム　約1/2個
スモークサーモン　50g
生鮭(切り身・皮つき)　110g
バター　5g
ケイパー　5g
サラダオイル、塩、こしょう　各適宜
ディル(飾り用)　適宜
＊ケイパーは、ペーパータオルの上で水分をきってから計量する。

準備(3種共通)
・天板にクッキングシートを敷いておく。
・オーブンを180℃に温める。

作り方

1 パート・ブリゼ・サレを5mm厚さにのばし、ピケ(多数)をして、直径6cmの菊型で6枚抜き、冷蔵庫で20分休ませた後、網をのせて20分焼き、網を取ってドレをして、さらに約10分オーブンで焼く。

2 ライムの果肉を取り出し(20g使用する。皮は残しておく。p.35参照)、5mm角に切る。スモークサーモンは5mm幅に切る。

3 フライパンにサラダオイルを入れて熱し、生鮭を入れてこしょうをし、ライムの皮をのせて焼く。熱いうちにほぐし、さらにフォークで押しくずして細かくする。とかしバターを加え、塩、こしょうで味を調える。

4 3が冷めたら2とケイパーを加えて混ぜ合わせ、1にのせてディルを飾る。

アヴォカド＋えび
Avocat＋crevettes

材料(4人分)

パート・ブリゼ・サレ　約100g	チャービル　適宜
アヴォカド　1個	マヨネーズ
えび　8尾	(お好みで)　適宜
日本酒、塩　各適宜	

作り方

1 パート・ブリゼ・サレを5mm厚さにのばし、ピケ(多数)をして、底辺4.5×高さ7cmの直角三角形を8枚切り、冷蔵庫で20分休ませた後、網をのせて、オーブンで約30分焼く。

2 えびは背わたを取り、日本酒と塩を入れた湯でゆで、自然に冷ましてから殻をむく。アヴォカドは好みの形に切り、1、えびとともに皿に盛りつけ、チャービルを飾り、お好みでマヨネーズを添える。

島本 薫（しまもと かおる）
4年半パリで暮らし、パリの「ル・コルドン・ブルー」でグラン・ディプロームを取得。「タイユヴァン」「ラデュレ」で修業し、食べ歩いたレストランは数知れず。帰国後、地元兵庫県宝塚市にて料理教室を開講。管理栄養士のころ培った、実験、知識に基づいた、理論を交えて楽しく作るフランス料理、お菓子クラスは人気。子ども会などへの出張料理教室も好評。著書に『憧れのパリ16区の日常』『アイスクリーム大好き！』『パウンドケーキ大好き』（すべて文化出版局刊）がある。
大人と子供のためのフランス菓子、フランス料理教室
「Petit à petit（プティ・タ・プティ）」
http://www.kaorushimamoto.com

皆さま、島本薫のオリジナルタルトをお楽しみいただけましたでしょうか？　今回も、スタイリング、撮影、執筆と、心を込めて進めてまいりました。ボロボロになるまで使っていただけましたら幸いです。この本を手に取ってくださった皆さま、カメラマンの田中陽子さん、デザイナーの鷲巣隆さん、文化出版局の並木信子さん。今回も、ご一緒することができたことに喜びを感じています。そして、食器を快く貸してくださった田中さんのお母さま、フランス語をご指導くださったOlivierとYoko。皆さまに感謝しております。Merci infiniment !

装丁、レイアウト　　鷲巣 隆
　　　　　　　　　　鷲巣デザイン事務所
撮影　　田中陽子

気軽に楽しむ
タルト大好き！

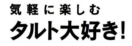

発　行　2006年11月19日　第1刷

著　者　島本　薫
発行者　大沼　淳
発行所　文化出版局
　　　　〒151-8524　東京都渋谷区代々木3-22-7
　　　　電話 03-3299-2565（編集）
　　　　　　 03-3299-2540（営業）
印刷所　株式会社文化カラー印刷
製本所　小髙製本工業株式会社

Ⓒ Kaoru Shimamoto 2006
Photographs Ⓒ Yoko Tanaka 2006
Printed in Japan

Ⓡ 本書の全部または一部を無断で複写（コピー）することは、
著作権法上での例外を除き、禁じられています。
本書からの複写を希望される場合は、日本複写権センター
（☎03-3401-2382）にご連絡ください。

お近くに書店がない場合、読者専用注文センターへ　☎0120-463-464
ホームページ　http://books.bunka.ac.jp/